Health Experts in the Media

Communication and Health Set

coordinated by
Laurence Corroy and Christelle Chauzal-Larguier

Volume 2

Health Experts in the Media

Between Legitimacy and Controversy

Edited by

Laurence Corroy
Christelle Chauzal-Larguier
Aurélie Pourrez

ISTE

WILEY

First published 2024 in Great Britain and the United States by ISTE Ltd and John Wiley & Sons, Inc.

ISTE Ltd
27-37 St George's Road
London SW19 4EU
UK

www.iste.co.uk

John Wiley & Sons, Inc.
111 River Street
Hoboken, NJ 07030
USA

www.wiley.com

Library of Congress Control Number: 2024939838

British Library Cataloguing-in-Publication Data
A CIP record for this book is available from the British Library
ISBN 979-1-78630-976-1

Contents

Author Presentation

Christelle Chauzal-Larguier

Christelle Chauzal-Larguier is an Associate Professor of Management Sciences at the Clermont Auvergne University and a member of the *Laboratoire communication et sociétés* (EA 4647). Her research focuses on corporate communication and corporate social responsibility (CSR), including solidarity policy, which she explored from the perspective of paid family caregivers and the schemes devised to help them[1].

Laurence Corroy

Laurence Corroy is a Professor of Information and Communication Sciences at the *Centre de recherche sur les médiations* (CREM, UR 3476) at the University of Lorraine. Her work focuses on two main areas of research: first, critical media literacy, including digital technology and information literacy, and the communicative practices of young people; second, health education, particularly how health issues are formed in the public arena, television dramas and by related media discourse and representations.

Stéphanie Debray

Stéphanie Debray got her PhD at the University of Lorraine and is an associate member of the Archives Henri-Poincaré – Philosophie et

1 Chauzal-Larguier, C. and Rouquette, S. (2018). *La solidarité, une affaire d'entreprise ?* Presses universitaires Blaise-Pascal, Clermont-Ferrand.

Recherches sur les Sciences et les Technologies (AHP-PReST) research team. Her thesis investigates the demarcation problem between scientific and non-scientific productions, and the question of values in science in the field of the philosophy of science. Her research focuses on the distinctions between science and pseudoscience, scientific misconduct and other dark practices. She holds a temporary teaching and research position at Gustave Eiffel University as part of the university's Information and Communication Sciences research team (2021–2023). Her dual disciplinary grounding enables her to study issues linked to the production, dissemination and impact of science in society, and to analyze its epistemic, methodological, communicational and organizational aspects, particularly where scientific activity involves different and competing actors (e.g. citizens, advocacy NGOs or industry representatives).

Valérie Delavigne

Valérie Delavigne is an Associate Professor in Linguistics at Sorbonne Nouvelle University and a member of the laboratory CLESTHIA (EA 7345). She has worked for several years with the Institut National du Cancer, which offers an information platform and for which she directed the online dictionary for patients. Concerned by linguistics in touch with reality, her research focuses on the uses and social circulation of terminologies and on the forms of scientific, technical and medical popularization, in line with research into socioterminology. She is currently working on a critical dictionary on ecology, while continuing her research into the language aspects of medical expertise.

Lucile Desmoulins

Lucile Desmoulins is an Associate Professor of Information and Communication Sciences at Gustave Eiffel University and a member of the DICEN-Idf research team. Her research focuses on ICS and cognitive approaches to public policy, more precisely the links between organizational communication and influence, lobbying as well as scientific advocacy strategies. She questions for instance the hybridity of organizational and managerial forms and discourse. She also studies the methods and tools of influencer marketing, notably, through the discursive and organizational dimensions of identity and authority in the digital age and social media. As the head of the master's program in business intelligence (BI), influence, lobbying and social media influence strategies (M2IE-ILMS), she analyzes the evolution of professional deontological standards and codes of ethics, focusing on dark BI and public relations digital methods and strategies.

Oihana Husson

Oihana Husson is a PhD candidate in Information and Communication Sciences at the University of Burgundy and a member of the CIMEOS (Communications, Mediations, Organizations, Knowledge, EA 4177) research unit. Her research focuses on healthcare expertise on social media and the professionalization of social media influencers.

Alexis Meyer

Alexis Meyer is the Manager of Bourbon-Lancy's Tourist and Spa Information Office (*Office de tourisme et du thermalisme*) and an Associate Professor/Lecturer at the Clermont Auvergne University. After studying strategic information and international market policy, he first worked in the marketing department of a Lyon-based retail group, before taking over the management of Bourbon-Lancy's Tourist and Spa Information Office. His research focuses mainly on institutional/corporate communications, with an emphasis on support in relation to strategies applied to the spa/wellness and tourism sectors.

Alexandra Micciche

Alexandra Micciche is a PhD student of Contemporary History at the Université Libre de Bruxelles (ULB) and the University of Namur, and works with ULB's *Mondes modernes et contemporains* (MMC) research center and the University of Namur's *Histoire, sons et images* (HiSI) research group. As part of her doctoral project, she is studying the mobilizations of medical and nursing staff in their relationship with Belgian public television programs between 1964 and 1989.

Aurélie Picton

Aurélie Picton has been an Associate Professor in the Department of Translation Technology (TIM) at the University of Geneva since 2011. She teaches terminology, lexicology and language resources, language for special purposes and the use of corpora for translation. She obtained her PhD in Linguistics in 2009 from the University of Toulouse, co-funded by the French National Centre for Scientific Research (Laboratoire CLLE-RSS, CNRS, UMR 5263) and the French National Centre for Space Studies (CNES). She is also an associate member of the *Observatoire de linguistique Sens-Texte* (OLST) at the University of Montreal. Her main research interests concern the analysis of dialectal variation in specialized discourse, from a textual and socioterminological perspective. She is also interested in the impact of technologies on the practice/s of language professionals (e.g. the ANR CRISTAL project, 2012–2016). Since 2005, she has been involved in a number of applied projects on terminological variation and term circulation, particularly in the fields of space, humanitarian studies, particle physics and medicine.

Sylvie Pierre

Sylvie Pierre is a Professor of Information and Communication Sciences at the *Centre de recherche sur les médiations* (CREM, UR 3476) at the University of Lorraine. Her main research interests concern the history, actor's strategies and ethical issues of television. In the past, she was the editor head of the health and education department at *La Cinquième Chaîne, Chaîne du savoir et de la connaissance* from 1994 to 1998.

Aurélie Pourrez

Aurélie Pourrez is an Associate Professor in information and communication sciences at the University of Lorraine and a researcher at the *Centre de recherche sur les médiations* (CREM, UR 3476). Her work focuses on health communication and environmental communication. She also works on the social, environmental and ethical responsibility of organizations, as well as on communication implemented for the safety and health of employees. She directs the ANR GwadaSafeMeat project to reduce chlordecone contamination in the population via the informal beef circuit in Guadeloupe.

Émilie Roche

Émilie Roche is an Associate Professor at the Sorbonne Nouvelle University's *Centre de recherche sur les liens sociaux* (CERLIS, UMR 8070). Her work examines the media coverage of violence (terrorism, war, urban and police violence), health, the environment and presidential campaigns.

Corinne Rochette

Corinne Rochette is a Professor at the Clermont Auvergne University's School of Management (IAE) and a member of its CleRMa (*Clermont recherche management*) research center. She designed a master's degree in Public Management, as well as one in the management of medico-social and healthcare organizations, and is co-founder and holder of the Health and Territories research chair of Clermont Auvergne University Foundation. She is Academic President of the International Association of Public Management Research and an expert for several public organizations, including the French Public Health Council. She studies the transformations of public organizations and services, as well as access to care, innovative organizational systems, governance and patient pathways. She is currently supervising six theses. Her research output amounts to some 100 academic contributions, including articles and conferences.

Baptiste Schummer

Baptiste Schummer is a PhD student in Political Science at the *Centre d'études de recherches administratives politiques et sociales* (CERAPS, UMR 8026) at the University of Lille. He is currently writing his thesis, under the supervision of Jean-Gabriel Contamin and Nicolas Kaciaf, comparing French media coverage of glyphosate and violence against women between 2000 and 2020. As an extension of his PhD project, he recently published an article, "*Le glyphosate et les journalistes en France: la construction sociale d'un problème public médiatisé (2000–2020)*", in the journal *Sur le journalisme*, Volume 11, no. 2, 2022. He has also published in the journal *Politiques de Communication*, "*Durer dans le champ médiatique. La carrière d'Alain Duhamel*", Volume 13, no. 2, 2019, which drew on his master's thesis on the sociology of journalism (Sciences Po Lille).

Emma Thibert

Emma Thibert has worked as a Research and Teaching Assistant at the Department of Translation Technology (TIM) at the University of Geneva since June 2019, after having completed her master's degree in Translation and Technology at the university's Faculty of Translation and Interpreting. She collaborated on the Humanitarian Encyclopedia project, coordinated by the Geneva Centre for Education and Research in Humanitarian Action (CERAH), before joining the university's terminology team, where she started working on her PhD thesis, under the supervision of Aurélie Picton (TIM-FTI) and Valérie Delavigne (CLESTHIA, Sorbonne Nouvelle University), in 2021. Her fields of interest are textual terminology, socioterminology, variation in specialty languages, corpus linguistics and term circulation.

Preface

For a long time, expertise has primarily been used by policy makers. They have made use of expertise to provide a "rational" basis for policy decisions. To this end, public health policies are no exception. The relationship between health authorities, as the holders of knowledge-based expertise, and the State, as the centralized power, has long been imbued with it, maintaining its ambiguous nature (Tabuteau 2010). In recent decades, the practice of consulting experts has become more widespread, and "the challenge of expertise is all the more problematic given that the term has become more used and widespread and that times have transformed the learned and professional institutions that gave the expert their title in the 18th and (especially) 19th centuries" (Berrebi-Hoffmann and Lallement 2009, p. 6). It is no longer solely public authorities or academic circles that lay claim to the figure of the expert; now, experts are widely consulted by the media, for the purpose of informing the public and making expertise publically available, which has sparked debate over the content of "expert" knowledge, and the role and place of these experts (Collins and Evans 2007). The practice of consulting experts "whose research focus is conditioned by the imperatives of action and reform" (Delmas 2011, p. 16) is thus aimed at new objectives.

The term "expert", deriving from the Latin *expertus*, means "one who has proven themselves". According to the *Dictionnaire de l'Académie* (1687), in the 17th century, an expert was defined as "well-versed in/adept at some art that can be learned by experience", such as surgery. At the same time, Richelet's dictionary defined an expert as a "savant, adept and accomplished

---

Preface written by Laurence CORROY and Christelle CHAUZAL-LARGUIER.

in something; experienced". This two-pronged meaning was more explicitly divided in the 19th century, as evident in *Littré* (1863): on the one hand, the expert refers to an individual "who has, through experience, acquired great skill in a profession" and, on the other, one "who, having acquired knowledge of certain things, is appointed to verify and decide on them". In the field of health, a distinction is made between expert appraisals, such as psychiatric appraisals, carried out by doctors, and psychological appraisals carried out by health professionals or medical specialists who are not doctors in a variety of circumstances (e.g. personal follow-up of the patient, legal cases, administrative litigation, etc.).

The expert and their expertise are the subject of increasing attention in academic research, giving rise to an abundance of publications. Researchers from various disciplinary fields have sought to gain a better understanding of expertise and have drawn on different approaches to develop methods of analysis, such as psychology and its individual approach, sociology opting for a more contextualized approach, or management sciences and their organizational angle. In information and communication sciences, researchers seek to understand the communicational, political and heuristic dynamics of the practice of consulting of experts, particularly by the media. Today, society's many developments in the field of health and communication are renewing interest in experts and the questions they arouse. This book sets out to examine in detail the widespread use of experts, who are positioned as informants, authority figures or interpreters of current events (Campion and Van Wynsberge 2017), by journalists, their presence in traditional and digital media and the pliable definition of expertise, among other issues.

The media coverage of health experts' words highlights the difficulty recipients have in assessing legitimacy and the trust that can be placed in them. There is an element of vagueness and ambivalence in the notion of expertise as it is conceptualized by the media that needs to be investigated further. This can be seen in examples of experts' (sometimes conflicting) opinions on recurring topics in public health – health crises, vaccinations, end of life care, chronic care pathways – as well as well-being-related matters and factors (sexuality, nutrition, environment, etc.) for a healthy life. The proliferation of the media, news channels and digital offerings, while at the same time the increase in life expectancy – which has doubled in the space of a century – poses new medical challenges, has led to a growing demand for expert advice, which in recent years has become increasingly complex and protean.

The very identity of the expert called upon to deal with medical issues is not self-evident, since real-life experience, scholarly knowledge or media coverage seem to justify their presence, depending on the case. Who qualifies as a health expert?

The complex figure of the health expert

The figure of the health expert, as consulted by the media, is neither subject to the same standards of transparency, nor required to meet the same criteria of competence as when they are consulted by policy makers (Joly 1999; Bérard and Crespin 2010). As such, the aim of this book is to study the health expert in the media in order to understand the complexity of their role, question their legitimacy and to better understand the controversies they can provoke. Generally speaking, legitimacy can be defined as a "generalized perception or supposition that an entity's actions are desirable, and appropriate within a socially-constructed system of norms, values, beliefs and meanings" (Suchman 1995, p. 574).

A person with a particular kind of institutionally recognized (and therefore legitimate) expertise may be presented as an expert in a completely different context. Today, the expert has many facets, adaptable or even shaped to suit the context, and can in turn take on "the features of the consultant proposing reforms", don "the clothes of the evaluator and auditor", propose indicators and assume "the role of the scientist" analyzing the risks incurred by the population (Berrebi-Hoffmann and Lallement 2009, p. 6). This can fuel mistrust or suspicion of manipulation of opinions[1], but it can also influence and, in some cases, overturn the relationship between the media and "experts". While the intent here is not necessarily to sway public opinion, the tendency to call on experts for matters that fall outside of their recognized field of expertise has led to the spread of a buzzword that has become fashionable since the Covid-19 pandemic: ultracrepidarianism, which involves giving our opinion on subjects despite lacking the

1 We can point to the manipulation of the Tobacco Industry Research Committee as the root of this mistrust. Dr. Clarence Cook Little was put in charge of the research group that was supposed to be studying the causality of tobacco in lung cancer, but he was actually receiving funding to study the genetic factor in the onset of cancer from 1959 to 1964.

competence to do so (Villain 2021). In academia, where research fields are becoming increasingly specific, this sudden interdisciplinarity vis-à-vis expertise may seem strange:

> Today, expertise is at the heart of public debate; it is at the heart of controversies that touch on broad social challenges connected to scientific, technical, and ethical issues. (Dumoulin 2013, p. 717)

Influencers who endorse products in the name of health expertise, despite being paid to do so by brands, are yet another example of this phenomenon.

It is worth considering how journalists go about consulting experts and the strategies they use. Major public health issues and successive health contexts have seen the multiplication of various, contradictory expert voices, summoned in contracted times (health crises linked to food, meteorological phenomena, an epidemic or a pandemic, exposure to a contaminating element, etc.), which may constitute an additional difficulty for journalists, particularly in terms of ethics. Indeed, these choices have the potential to influence the way in which a major public health problem can become a public health problem. Yet, it remains unclear whether these strategies are profoundly different from those generally used by the press, and what verification tools journalists mobilize on this occasion (Bigot 2017). The processing of scientific news, its hierarchization, the ways in which journalists mobilize enunciative procedures to get researchers and doctors to talk, as well as the way in which the words of experts are requested, presented and used, are all pressing issues.

Journalists specialized in the field of healthcare journalism have been able to claim, or they have been granted, the qualification of health expert, and in this capacity they have worked as consultants on TV or in other media, which have not explained the career trajectory and prior training of these journalists (Comby 2009). In such cases, would the term "consultant" not be more accurate than "expert" to describe journalists of this profile? On the other hand, a small number of doctors and researchers are regularly invited to take on the role of columnists or even TV directors. For Gérald Kierzek, an emergency doctor who is used to appearing on television:

> [D]octors on television have the necessary legitimacy, acquired beyond their title, through their practice. This proximity to care

> and patients seems to be an important condition for a discourse that makes sense and is connected to the field. It is also a rare but interesting career move for practitioners locked into rigid and unattractive curricula, whether in hospital or the private sector, or quite simply a breath of fresh air for more occasional appearances that allow them to showcase their work or research. (Kierzek 2023)

The boundary between health journalists and medical journalists is becoming porous, and the presentation of each other's legitimacy as health experts is not universally accepted and recognized.

While the media offers an ever-expanding space for expression, including everyone's personal opinion on a health topic, which can be easily and widely shared online, this does not make everyone an expert and their opinions real expertise (Prior 2003) – a term that is now widely "overused" (Bernard 2022). Nevertheless, new forms of expertise are emerging, particularly on the Internet.

Forms of expertise in healthcare

According to Grimaldi (2010, p. 92), "[t]he scientific expert is not only a scientist, but also an experienced person who has mastered the multiple facets of their field of expertise, is aware of their limits, and is able to call on complementary expertise". Alongside doctors and professional carers, a wide variety of non-professional stakeholders involved in healthcare processes are now taking the floor. Whether they are peer caregivers, expert caregivers, expert patients, expert users, etc., their place is growing within healthcare establishments, where they are recognized as a form of expertise. The "expert patient" (Shaw and Baker 2004; Lindsay and Vrijhoef 2009) and, more recently, other lay experts, such as non-professional caregivers, are the focus of increasing attention in scientific research, although the bounds of their expertise remain largely unexplored.

Other types of actors – such as influencers, associations, groups of patients or relatives, road accident victims, victims of industrial accidents, etc. – also hold a form of healthcare expertise, and can act as whistleblowers by helping to mobilize public opinion and generate media coverage of a health cause, which can in turn lead the State to better consider, or even recognize, urgent social issues (e.g. occupational illness, drug poisoning, prevention, etc.).

However, the media coverage of complementary expertise remains confidential, and the role played by doctors is no stranger to this, as "the change from a paternalistic to a deliberative model modifies the status of the doctor and leads to resistance on their part, consciously or unconsciously, to these changes and to the changes they imply (notably in their own behaviors) in order to preserve the asymmetry of knowledge, the basis of their power" (Boudier et al. 2012). In other words, doctors, or more generally professional caregivers, are reluctant to share their healthcare expertise in the media. Could this stem from a fear of seeing their power and authority, and therefore their legitimacy, compromised in a Weberian sense?

As someone with scientific knowledge, a doctor is recognized as legitimate and legitimized in making decisions concerning the best course of treatment for a given patient[2]. However, their expert judgment cannot be considered absolute. Although some doctors have become accustomed to the exercise of communication in the media (such as Professor Salomon and Professor Raoult), this expertise is shaken up, even contested and, in certain ultimate cases, challenged, as recent examples relating to vaccination or the treatment of certain cancers can attest, reinforcing the conception of Habermasian legitimacy according to which the latter arises as the result "of general deliberation" (Habermas 1973, p. 180). The risk taken by legitimate experts in the media is all the greater as their field of expertise is expanded and fragmented on the Internet, and any form of discourse can be commented on and directly challenged.

Traditional and digital media also serve as a sounding board for patients and their families, who have developed a form of expertise through their own experiences of health conditions. This expertise, of a different nature, is described as "lay" and often recognized as complementary to "academic" expertise (Massé 2012). Research has highlighted the necessary coexistence of the two (McClean and Shaw 2005), but this supposes that the context of coexistence leaves a clear field of expression to each. An acceptable definition would include people with no academic training in the area of health about which they are expressing themselves (Salman and Topçu 2015). For Barbaras (1998), knowledge gained through experience cannot be generalized given the contextual specificities in which it was acquired, thus echoing Popper's (1991) distinction between knowledge specific to each individual and acquired through personal experience, and scientific

2 French Council of State order of July 26, 2017.

knowledge that is recognized by the community, shared by a collective and transmissible as is, extending beyond the individual.

The "lay" expert holds what is generally referred to as experiential knowledge of their own situation (Simon et al. 2020), just like the "experienced consumer" (Leveratto 2021) or the "ordinary public" who develops a particular appetence (Rouquette 2021). The concept of experiential knowledge, coined by Borkman (1976), is not without confusion (Hejoaka et al. 2019). The lay expert may serve as a possible resource for the patient who lacks medical and therapeutic knowledge of their own health condition (Bolam et al. 2003). Here, let us make a clear distinction between experience and expertise: while "the patient is increasingly recognized and used as an expert who has acquired their expertise through experience" (Jouet 2009, p. 47), to be an expert, "they must be able to communicate, to explain clearly without distorting information, and to be pedagogical" (Friconneau et al. 2020, p. 62). This makes all the difference.

But as soon as a group of "laypeople" are accompanied by a medical professional or involved in a scientific committee, the expert opinion becomes "half-lay, half-professional", producing "a counter-expertise" (Grimaldi 2010, p. 91). Some patients' associations, thanks to the quality of their field studies and research, have been able to assert their expertise in the healthcare field (Dalgalarrondo 2007). When a "lay" expert shares their knowledge, questions remain as to how to communicate, the media chosen to do so and the targets of their discourse. At another level, it is the legitimacy of speaking out in the public arena, and the power this gives them to exercise, deserve to be explained. At a time when everyone can share their experiences and advice on the Internet, digital social networks play an important role, enabling forms of resistance to the dominant medical discourse to flourish (Aka Miézan 2022).

This book intends to share work relating to the processes of media legitimation or delegitimization of expert figures, to the evolution of the mediatization processes of scientific knowledge, or even to the political game, tacit or not, institutional experts requested. Does the media presence of health experts influence institutional discourse, decision-making and the implementation of health policy in France (Akrich and Rabeharisoa 2012)? How do the different actors express themselves on health issues (Chopyak and Levesque 2002)? And with what regime of truth and controversy? This work, with contributions from researchers from across the humanities and social sciences, offers elements of answers by presenting in a first part works that analyze media controversies of experts, then in a second the conflict of expertise lay people and scientists in the media.

Experts in media controversies

Stéphanie Debray and Lucile Desmoulins examine the discourses and expert figures involved in the marketing of dapoxetine, a drug initially used for the treatment of anxiety disorders, but which is now authorized in some countries to treat premature ejaculation and thus improve sexual well-being. They question the ambiguous legal and medical status of a drug, which is authorized in France, but remains banned in the US and appears on a reference list of drugs to be avoided, as published by the world's leading independent health journal. The originality of their investigation lies in its multi-disciplinary theoretical and methodological grounding, which draws on information and communication sciences, the philosophy of science and agnotology.

Stéphanie Debray and Lucile Desmoulins analyze a multi-media public relations campaign (featuring posters, TV commercials, advertisements in the press, internal sites apparently of general interest, including the particular case of a "digital clinic") in order to bring to light the strategies of obscure communication, "ambiguous" and unknown to the public. Medical literature and meta-analyses enrich the corpus of investigation. By simultaneously seeking to examine the relationships between experts and commercial organizations, the investigation also falls within the field of the epistemology of ignorance. It reaffirms and questions the subtle distinction between links of interest and conflicts of interest. Debray and Desmoulins open, so to speak, the black box of a global communication strategy that makes it possible to influence several types of audience and to promote the sale of a drug discretely.

Baptiste Schummer centers his study around another type of influence, and analyzes the ways in which a public health problem is tackled journalistically by opinions pre-existing journalists on the subject, through the case of glyphosate over the period 2000–2020. Journalists may or may not consider this to be a serious public health problem. Expertise seems, in this context, less able to control and animate the controversy than to represent a resource that can be mobilized according to the expectations of those who request it. The author evokes the cosmetic function of the objectivity of expertise, as well as its plasticity, which can be used by journalists for the use of glyphosate, or conversely by its detractors, by mobilizing dissident experts. In this case, experts thus serve as scientific guarantors for journalists previously ideologically convinced of the safety or dangerousness of glyphosate, and, by extension, confirm their support or lack thereof for a particular institutional and political stance.

Sylvie Pierre examines the choice of expert consulted for a health TV program in light of its objectives. She studies the case of *L'Amour en questions* (1994–1998), a program dedicated in France to sex education on a public television channel with the objective of promoting knowledge and awareness. By drawing on her past experience as a program editor, she is able to enrich her analysis of discourse and devices with an empirical perspective. Allowing viewers to adopt free and enlightened behavior imposed a production logic mobilizing the ethical principles of autonomy and responsibility. The decision to consult Professor Étienne-Émile Baulieu, inventor of the abortion pill (RU-486), as the expert and scientific guarantor of the television program, raises questions as to his status as a doctor as well as the objectives pursued by the creators of the show. In association with the pharmaceutical industry that tested, produced and marketed RU-486, Prof. Baulieu had to specify the existing link of interest in his report with the laboratory. Beyond the controversy surrounding the doctor's potential economic interest, it was above all an ideological controversy that provoked divergent reactions. The show, wishing to transmit knowledge and disseminate an emancipatory and feminist discourse on the subject of sexuality – at the heart of ideological and political tensions – uses the expert as a figure of authority, as well as an opinion leader.

In Belgium, a task force for medical reform responsible for initiating or supporting health policy reforms has, over several decades, pursued a strategy of entryism vis-à-vis the media in order to communicate with the public. Alexandra Micciche recounts the group's atypical trajectory from the 1960s to the 1990s, which ensured the diffusion of its sociopolitical vision of healthcare by hiring, among others, a journalist as the communications manager. From an informal think-tank, it has become the standard-bearer of medical dissidence in Belgium, striking a chord with the academic, medical and citizen worlds. The media's quarrels over values with the medical establishment thus occupied the Belgian public discourse. The decriminalization of abortion, the status of the mentally ill and health education were debated, provoking major controversies. At the height of its popularity, the group was recognized as an official organization for continuing education, before suffering budget cuts, which limited its activities to the participation of volunteers, until it merged with the *Fédération des maisons médicales*. The analysis of the media coverage of this allows us to outline several concomitant developments in terms of publication and mediation of medicine and health in the second half of the 20th century. The mirror image of the Belgian expert's stratification episode begs the question of how public service media could more clearly take on the role of institutional intermediary.

The second half of this book takes a closer look at the status of lay expertise in comparison to scientific expertise, and reflects on their similar and opposing aspects.

Lay expertise versus scientific expertise

The historian Yvonne Knibiehler notes that in the 20th century, when women entered a clinic for childbirth, they were placed under the care of doctors. A century later, in a societal context in which the issue of obstetric violence and women's testimonies are increasingly significant, the portrayal of the ethos of an expert doctor, gynecologist, in magazines targeting families with young children is the subject of study by Laurence Corroy and Émilie Roche. The chronicle signed by the head of the clinic is interesting both for what it expresses about the status of the expert practitioner and the representations he has of his role and his knowledge, and for what he cannot help saying, almost in spite of himself. At once a caregiver, practitioner, expert and godlike figure, the gynecologist's real or imagined omnipotence comes up against, if not resistance from women, at least a desire to provoke a conversation about pregnancy and women's bodies.

The asymmetrical relationship that clearly emerges in the discourse reported by the expert chronicler reveals an injunctive and normative discourse of a knowing figure facing his patients. This medical expertise, as it is presented in these magazines, raises questions of gender inequalities in the patient/doctor relationship, with the expert testifying to their symbolic and effective omnipotence over the bodies of parturients. This dominant position raises the question – Is it desirable, or even tenable? – while the horizontality of the Internet is swarming with testimonies and patient associations who ask to be at least consulted on and associated with care protocols.

While family caregivers are becoming an increasingly important part of the public discourse, even in the election platforms of high-level politicians, they are not among the health expert figures often called upon by the media, because their expertise is widely perceived to lack conviction and legitimacy. Christelle Chauzal-Larguier and Alexis Meyer are interested in the legitimacy granted to the expertise of the caregiver in current media and analyze caregiver figures who have managed to appear in certain media sporadically, in the way in which these are perceived and the organizational effort implemented (associations, online forums) to find support and finally be heard by the media. Numerous, unknown and sometimes little recognized by state services, caregivers must find ways to make their voices heard so that they can promote policy change to make their daily lives easier. Is there greater media interest in the expertise of caregivers? Is it sufficiently considered and understood? If research works risk using the term expertise in this regard, the warning relating to the popularization of knowledge is raised. Indeed, caregivers have acquired experience through their personal situation, to which they can speak, but rarely can they be categorized as lay experts wishing and/or able to communicate in the media with the necessary critical distance and the valorization of more general and transposable experiential knowledge.

Corinne Rochette examines the process of legitimizing patient expertise, based on the steps taken by an association of patients with persistent symptoms of Covid-19 infection, the *ApresJ20* association. The actions of the patients themselves, leading to recognition of their expertise, express the empowerment that has been transforming the healthcare field in recent years. The lay knowledge that patients have of their symptoms and illness from their day-to-day experience constitutes valuable knowledge, particularly in the context of new health situations, but it requires legitimization in order to be accepted by society. Society's recognition of lived experience requires patients to develop critical distance.

Rochette discusses the process of legitimization that leads to recognition of patients' expertise, based on the sociopolitical and pragmatic–cognitive dimensions of legitimacy and legitimization strategies. Based on an analysis of the content of the communication of an association of so-called "long Covid" patients, this chapter leads to a modeling of the process of recognizing the expertise of these patients around four stages. This case study highlights how the digital media acts as a catalyst in this regard.

Oihana Husson explores one of the new figures of lay expertise: health influencers. Suffering from various chronic or long-term conditions, they have become experts on their own bodies, as they share their care journey online. Influencer marketing strategies can utilize their popularity. The Internet and, more particularly, Web 2.0, thus plays a key role by adding a social and economic component. Valorization of a life journey, monetization of lay expertise, the case of patient influencers raises ethical and scientific questions in that it escapes the traditional circuit of recognition of scholarly expertise. Galvanized by the echo that their words find on social networks, these influencers of a new type are keen to maintain the interest and loyalty of followers and to constantly develop their image capital that they exploit.

Some even manage to occupy a prominent place among the most talked-about lay health experts. Sharing their lay expertise with the widest possible audience affords them legitimacy, which they then nurture through their increasingly meticulous creation of published content. The health influencer may be tempted to position themselves as a peer, and to propose, or even prescribe (in the sense of suggesting a course of action), a treatment, and therefore to grant themselves a strategic role between the patient follower and their doctor. While their lay expertise as it pertains to their own situation is legitimate, it is much more controversial in peer assistance.

From expertise and its recognition, to illnesses and their definition, Emma Thibert, Aurélie Picton and Valérie Delavigne remind us that the terms used to describe them are not anecdotal. The authors chose to focus on the field of diabetology, a pilot specialty in therapeutic education. Insulin therapy has, in fact, allowed for a century a chronicization of diabetes, which until then was lethal. A study of specialized discourses in diabetology, using data from written productions and real-life situations, will help us to better understand whether the various players involved are using the same concepts and the same lexical field. Through linguistic analysis, the authors are able to highlight patterns of similarity in this regard, as well as differences, and the linguistic specificities of the expert patients. When the terms used by health experts are used appropriately by patients, this helps to legitimize the hypothesis of lay expertise in the medical field. When coupled with terminology specific to the patient, it is evident that lay expertise combines a certain degree of academic expertise with a different way of caregivers talking about care and illness. This innovative approach offers a method that can be adapted to other areas, by addressing the question of lay expertise through the terminology used.

The different media-covered fields of expertise blur both definitions of expertise, as well as those of controversy (Chavot and Masseran 2023). Scientific controversy between peers is rarely staged publicly for its own sake; on the contrary, it turns out to be disturbed most often by the intervention of other actors and other non-academic experts who are caught together in the trap of a media system that they sometimes have little or no control over. As a controversial actor in this space, the health expert risks becoming the subject of controversy, with the media arena appearing in turn as a legitimizing or delegitimizing instance within which the public is increasingly taking part. The expert consulted by the media therefore poses major scientific, democratic and political challenges.

June 2024

References

Aka Miezan, B. (2022). Enjeux info-communicationnels dans la prévention des maladies chroniques en Côte d'Ivoire de 2011 à 2019. PhD Thesis, Université de Grenoble Alpes, Grenoble.

Akrich, M. and Rabeharisoa, V. (2012). L'expertise profane dans les associations de patients, un outil de démocratie sanitaire. *Santé Publique*, 24(1), 69–74.

Barbaras, R. (1998). *Le tournant de l'expérience : recherches sur la philosophie de Merleau-Ponty*. J. Vrin, Paris.

Bérard, Y. and Crespin, R. (eds) (2010). *Aux frontières de l'expertise. Dialogue entre savoirs et pouvoirs*. Presses Universitaires de Rennes, Rennes.

Bernard, F. (2017). Imaginaire, participation, engagement et empowerment. *Communication et organisation*, 45(1), 87–98.

Bernard, M.H. (2022). L'expertise en santé : quel devenir. *Annales Médico-psychologiques, revue psychiatrique*, 180(1), 57–59.

Berrebi-Hoffmann, I. and Lallement, M. (2009). À quoi servent les experts ? *Cahiers internationaux de sociologie*, 1(126), 5–12.

Bigot, L. (2018). Fact-checking. *Publictionnaire* [Online]. Available at: http://publictionnaire.huma-num.fr/notice/fact-checking [Accessed 26 February 2018].

Bolam, B., Gleeson, K., Murphy, S. (2003). Lay person or health expert? Exploring theoretical and practical aspects of reflexivity in qualitative health research. *Forum Qualitative Social Research*, 4(2). doi: 10.17169/fqs-4.2.699.

Borkman, T. (1976). Experiential knowledge: A new concept for the analysis of self-help groups. *Social Service Review*, 50(3), 445–456.

Boudier, F., Bensebaa, F., Jablanczy, A. (2012). L'émergence du patient-expert : une perturbation innovante. *Innovations*, 3(39), 13–25.

Bouquet, B. (2014). La complexité de la légitimité. *Vie Sociale*, 8, 13–23.

Campion, B. and Van Wynsberghe, C. (2017). Experts médiatiques. *La Revue Nouvelle*, 3, 26–29 [Online]. Available at: https://www.cairn.info/revue-nouvelle-2017-3-page-26.htm.

Chavot, P. and Masseran, A. (2023). Controverse publique (sociologie des sciences) [Online]. Available at: https://publictionnaire.huma-num.fr/wp-content/uploads/2016/10/controverse-publique.pdf.

Chopyak, J. and Levesque, P. (2002). Public participation in science and technology decision making: Trends for the future. *Technology in Society*, 24(1), 155–166.

Collins, H. and Evans, R. (2007). *Rethinking Expertise*. The University of Chicago Press, London.

Comby, J.B. (2009). Quand l'environnement devient médiatique. Conditions et effets de l'institutionnalisation d'une spécialité journalistique. *Réseaux*, 5/6(157/158), 157–190.

Dalgalarrondo, S. (2007). Quelle place pour les associations de malades dans le processus d'innovation médicamenteuse ? Le cas des maladies rares. *Revue française des affaires sociales*, 3(3/4), 171–191.

Delmas, C. (2011). *Sociologie politique de l'expertise*. La Découverte, Paris.

Dumoulin, L. (2013). L'expertise reproblématisée. *Droit et Société*, 3(85), 717–723.

Friconneau, M., Archer, A., Malaterre, J., Salama, F., Ouillade, M.C. (2020). Le patient-expert. Un nouvel acteur clé du système de santé. *Médecine/Sciences*, 36(2), 62–64.

Grimaldi, A. (2010). Les différents habits de "l'expert profane". *Les tribunes de la santé*, 2(27), 91–100.

Habermas, J. (1973). *La technique et la science comme idéologie*. Gallimard, Paris.

Hejoaka, F., Simon, E., Halloy, A., Arborio, S. (eds) (2019). Définir les savoirs expérientiels en santé : une revue de la littérature en sciences humaines et sociales. In *Les savoirs expérientiels en santé : fondements épistémologiques et enjeux identitaires*. Presses universitaires de Nancy, Nancy.

Henry, E., Gilbert, C., Jouzel, J. and Marichalar, P. (2015). *Dictionnaire critique de l'expertise. Santé, travail, environnement*. Presses de Sciences Po, Paris.

Joly, P.B. (1999). Besoin d'expertise et quête d'une légitimité nouvelle : quelles procédures pour réguler l'expertise scientifique ? *Revue française des affaires sociales*, 1, 45–53.

Jouet, E. (2009). Le savoir expérientiel dans le champ de la santé mentale : le projet Emilia. *Recherches en communication*, 32, 35–52.

Kierzek, G. (2023). Médecins et télévision. *Les Tribunes de la santé*, 75(1), 59–69.

Leveratto, J.M. (2021). Public expert. *Publictionnaire* [Online]. Available at: http://publictionnaire.huma-num.fr/notice/public-expert [Accessed 1 June 2021].

Lindsay, S. and Vrijhoef, H.J.M. (2009). Sociological focus on "expert patients". *Health Sociology Review*, 18, 139–144. doi: 10.5172/hesr.18.2.139.

Massé, R. (2012). Expertises éthiques savantes et profanes en santé publique : défis et enjeux pour une éthique de la discussion. *Santé Publique*, 24(1), 49–61.

McClean, S. and Shaw, A. (2005). From schism to continuum? The problematic relationship between expert and lay knowledge – An exploratory conceptual synthesis of two qualitative studies. *Qualitative Health Research*, 15(6), 729–749.

Popper, K.R. (1991). *La connaissance objective*. Aubier, Paris.

Prior, L. (2003). Belief, knowlede and expertise: The emergence of the lay expert in medical sociology. *Sociology of Health & Illness*, 25(3), 41–57.

Rouquette, S. (2021). Public ordinaire (radio, télévision). *Publictionnaire* [Online]. Available at: http://publictionnaire.huma-num.fr/notice/public-ordinaire-radio-television [Accessed 23 August 2021].

Salman, S. and Topçu, S. (2015). Expertise profane. In *Dictionnaire critique de l'expertise. Santé, travail, environnement*, Henry, E., Gilbert, C., Jouzel, J.N., Marichalar, P. (eds). Presses de Sciences Po, Paris.

Shaw, J. and Baker, M. (2004). Expert patient, dream or nightmare? *British Medical Journal*, 328, 723–724.

Simon, E., Arborio Halloi, A., Hejoaka, F. (eds) (2020). *Les savoirs expérientiels en santé. Fondements épistémologiques et enjeux identitaires*. Presses universitaires de Lorraine, Nancy.

Suchman, M.C. (1995). Managing legitimacy: Strategic and institutional approaches. *Academy of Management Review*, 20(3), 571–610.

Tabuteau, D. (2010). L'expert et la décision en santé publique. *Les tribunes de la santé*, 2(27), 33–48.

Villain, N. (2021). Ultracrépidarianisme, biais cognitifs et Covid-19 : année 2, impact et retour du savoir. *Revue de neuropsychologie*, 13(2), 127–128.

Weber, M. (1971). *Économie et société*. Plon, Paris.

PART 1

Experts Involved in Public Health Controversies

1

The Pharmaceutical Treatment of Premature Ejaculation: "Gray-Zone Communication"

1.1. Introduction

Dapoxetine[1], marketed under the brand name Priligy®, was initially developed by the pharmaceutical company Eli Lilly and Company as a selective serotonin reuptake inhibitor (SSRI) for treating anxiety disorders. The short duration of action of this substance makes it unsuitable for use as an antidepressant. After Johnson & Johnson bought dapoxetine, it was submitted as a New Drug Application to the U.S. Food and Drug Administration (FDA) in 2004 for the treatment of premature ejaculation (PE). To this day, the FDA has still not approved its application, and in 2005 issued a letter of non-approval stating that they require additional clinical data on both the drug's efficacy and safety. Since 2009, however, its use for treating PE has been approved by the competent authorities in many European countries, including Sweden, Finland, Austria, Portugal, Germany, Italy and Spain. In 2013, The French National Authority for Health

---

Chapter written by Stéphanie DEBRAY and Lucile DESMOULINS.

1 On this, see, for example: McMahon, C.G. (2012). The author of this article has been linked to several medical societies, and all of his numerous articles on the subject value dapoxetine as "an effective and safe treatment for PE and a major medical advance in sexual health", as the aforementioned article concludes.

authorized the pharmaceutical company, Menarini Group, to place Priligy on the market[2]. Meanwhile, the French journal *Prescrire* (2013, 2021) argued that dapoxetine's efficacy was too limited to justify its side effects. As of 2022, *Prescrire* still included Priligy, the brand name of dapoxetine, on its list of drugs to avoid.

This chapter combines approaches from philosophy of science, agnotology, and information and communication science to investigate the differing views held by countries, on the one hand, and experts, on the other. Our first hypothesis affirms the controversial nature of the status of Priligy and its prescription, despite numerous studies that testify to a therapeutic effectiveness that is as real as it is conditional. Second, expertise here would not be a relational situation of authority and trust, but rather a simulacrum in which a certain number of actors would find it beneficial to adhere to or participate in. We assess the "level of darkness" of communication on dapoxetine. Dark communication may be black, i.e. illegal, or different shades of gray, for different levels of ethical unacceptability (Dulek and Campbell 2015; Carayol et al. 2019; Desmoulins 2017, 2019).

Philosophy of science made it possible to analyze a wide medical literature to rule on the therapeutic efficacy of the treatment, as well as PE's status as a disease/pathology, and dapoxetine's status as a drug: Is dapoxetine really a therapeutic treatment, or does it belong to the wellness field? The scientific literature was considered not only in the context of a classical state-of-the-art review, but also as a crucial part of the research corpus. We did a comparative analysis of the studies' methodologies. The aim was to understand the extent to which the marketing and prescribing of dapoxetine was or was not considered controversial. The research took into account the meta-analyses published exhaustively on PubMed (18 meta-analyses)[3]. We drew on the philosophy of science literature on the

---

2 Pharmacotherapeutic class – ATC code: G04BX14. PRILIGY 30 mg and 60 mg, film-coated tablet containing the active substance dapoxetine. See: https://base-donnees-publique.medicaments.gouv.fr/. Other countries, including Russia, Malaysia, the Philippines, Argentina, Uruguay, Australia, New Zealand and South Korea, have also authorized its prescription.

3 The keywords used were "dapoxetine" and "premature ejaculation". The "Meta-Analysis" filter was then added. See: https://pubmed.ncbi.nlm.nih. gov/?term=dapoxetine+premature+ejaculation&filter=pubt.meta-analysis.

demarcation problem between science, pseudoscience and unacceptable forms of science, and agnotology or the epistemology of ignorance, in order to question conflicts and links of interest shared by researchers and commercial organizations, as well as to examine funding sources.

Drawing on information and communication science, our corpus also included a range of public communication materials from 2012 to 2015, as well as media statements. These included press and television advertisements[4], a promotional site disguised as an awareness-raising site (garderlecontrole.fr), an advertising infographic (an infomercial not identified as such) published in the national daily press (Chapman and Beltramini 2000), the website of the charles.co digital clinic, which includes a blog, a telemedicine offer and links to several accounts on digital social media platforms, and an Opinion Way survey conducted in 2013.

The Opinion Way survey highlighted that: 1) the prescription of dapoxetine for the treatment of PE is ambiguous on several levels – semantic and conceptual, therapeutic, etiological and categorical; 2) the communication strategy around dapoxetine makes use of a variety of media genres to reach a wide range of audiences, including physicians, general practitioners and psychiatrists who are encouraged to prescribe the drug, as well as psychologists who are encouraged to view PE from a purely mechanical and chemical angle; 3) the communication materials and strategies for the promotion of dapoxetine worked as a coherent whole thanks to the words of experts who participated in constructing a health problem, constructing frames of thought and imaginaries, social demands, ultimately helping to achieve the commercial objective of increasing drug sales.

1.2. The ambiguities and controversies regarding dapoxetine

1.2.1. *Semantic ambiguities surrounding PE*

Critical discourse is rare but powerful in the press review, with two articles in France's leading independent drug journal, *Prescrire*. Comparative analysis of the discourse in *Prescrire* (2013, 2021) and the 18 meta-analyses included in the corpus showed that the prescription of

4 See: http://www.culturepub.fr/videos/les-laboratoies-menarini-garder-le-controle/.

dapoxetine for the treatment of PE can be regarded as a controversial issue (the prescription, not the drug), regardless of the debates on pseudosciences (Debray 2022). Dapoxetine is an active substance whose therapeutic efficacy has been attested by clinical studies – unlike, for example, homeopathic capsules. It is controversial because of its diversely ambiguous nature.

"Ambiguous" can describe the vague or approximate aspect of a statement, but it can also refer to a subject lying between two categories, or to a term that has several meanings or interpretations. In our case, several forms of ambiguity are subtly intertwined and contribute to the controversy.

The semantic ambiguity of PE stems from the fact that both the term and the concept remain largely ill-defined. In the mass media[5] – which is more easily accessible to the public than the scientific literature – PE is presented as a sexual problem of the order of a disorder or dysfunction, with the emphasis on sexual dissatisfaction: intercourse is perceived to be too short, and does not conform to norms, while ejaculation is considered to be too rapid, and needs to be delayed or brought under control. From a medical point of view, PE is distinct from erectile dysfunction (ED) and simple dissatisfaction (subjective PE). Each requires different therapeutic treatments and specific clinical management. The DSM-5 and the International Society of Sexual Medicine (2013) define PE based on an intravaginal ejaculatory latency time (IELT) of less than one minute after penetration. Dapoxetine is recommended for long-term or recurrent PE (IELT < two minutes)[6], yet, this has been subtly erased by the indirect advertising discourse of the laboratory that markets this substance in France. Other leading online information platforms, those that are widely used but not always entirely reputable, and websites have only added to the confusion by setting this time limit at five minutes or even longer. Epidemiological data circulated by a number of French doctors and "experts", and subsequently the national media, are systematically overestimated. For example, the "digital clinic" website, charles.co, which aims to help "men obtain reliable information about their sexual problems", suggests that "20% to 30% of men are affected by

5 See: https://www.topsante.com/couple-et-sexualite/sexualite/troubles-sexuels-chez-l-homme/garderlecontrole.com-un-site-sur-l-ejaculation-precoce-31865; https://www.passeportsante.net/fr/Maux/Problemes/Fiche.aspx?doc=ejaculation-precoce.

6 In this article, the acronym PE does indeed refer to lifelong premature ejaculation (LLPE) or recurrent acquired premature ejaculation (APE) – in contradiction with the misleading usage favored by Menarini to promote the prescription of Priligy.

premature ejaculation"[7]. Yet, the prevalence of PE may not exceed 5% (Althof et al. 2014). The highest numbers for the prevalence of PE come from statistical data based on meta-analyses that compare studies which do not use the same definition or criteria. The data that minimizes the prevalence of PE the most are based on the most widely held definitions of PE (DSM-V, ISSM). Exaggerated figures lead the public to believe that PE is more common than it is, thus encouraging many men to consider themselves as being sick and curable (internalization of a so-called pathological state).

1.2.2. *Therapeutic and etiological ambiguities surrounding dapoxetine*

The vast majority of randomized trials[8] and meta-analyses show that dapoxetine has strong or moderate therapeutic efficacy at safe doses (30 mg or 60 mg), i.e. an acceptable benefit–risk ratio. A priori, therefore, there would be no controversy. However, the journal *Prescrire* (2013, 2021) published articles and brief reviews that were critical of dapoxetine. It also published a "black list" of "drugs to avoid in order to improve care"[9], which states that "the limited efficacy is not sufficient to justify its adverse effects, [...] disproportionate adverse effects", and that "the EU health authority should have refused its marketing authorization". These positions are based on a number of factors, which also came to light during the investigation.

Some argue that the therapeutic mechanism of dapoxetine is unclear (Clément et al. 2012), resulting in therapeutic ambiguity: dapoxetine may be effective, but it is not clear how. Studies are also subject to methodological bias. Feys (2015), for example, draws attention to numerous conflicts of interest; others point to a potential industry bias since studies funded by the treatment producer are likely to receive preferential treatment (Waldinger

7 We will examine this company and its various media in more detail later in this chapter. The site also features articles with click-bait titles: "3 exercises to last longer in bed", "Want to last longer in bed? 6 tips from a sexologist". The site also promotes Priligy for the treatment of PE. See: https://www.charles.co/.

8 To our knowledge, only one document, a *Science Médicale* thesis, directly challenges the therapeutic efficacy of dapoxetine for the treatment of PE: Feys, F. (2015).

9 In 2022, 14 lists for 14 specialties were published, along with details of the "reliable, rigorous and independent" research methods used to compile them. See: https://prescrire.org/fr/202/1834/55640/0/PositionDetails.aspx.

and Schweitzer 2008). Sexual medicine is one of the fields in which relationships between scientists and pharmaceutical companies are very close (Jannini et al. 2010). The most prolific authors of journal articles on PE often mention their "conflicting interests" in the methodology sections of their papers, given their activities as consultants and conference speakers for major pharmaceutical companies, including Menarini[10]. These experts, in light of their industry associations, act on several levels: they produce and disseminate clinical recommendations by publishing articles, by being at the head of specialized journals and professional associations, as well as by being the most quoted since they cite each other. In addition, they produce recommendations for testing the efficacy of dapoxetine in randomized controlled trials (RCTs).

Moreover, therapeutic ambiguity is linked to etiological ambiguity: PE can have several causes and is multifactorial. However, the nature of these causes remains unclear and subject to debate. Some studies see PE as a neurobiological or hereditary phenomenon (Waldinger 2002; Sangkum et al. 2013), whereas others point to pharmacological or urological causes, or thyroid problems (Sangkum et al. 2013). A considerable number of studies focus more on psychosocial causes. This lack of clarity as to the main causes of PE may affect the status of PE as a disease, and that of dapoxetine as an appropriate treatment: if PE is primarily a disorder caused by psychosocial determinants, would psycho-behavioral treatments devoid of side effects be more appropriate, as recommended by *Prescrire* (2013)? By presenting PE as an illness unrelated to the psyche, doctors and consultants are legitimizing the prescription of a drug treatment, in this case, Priligy, which is the only oral treatment authorized in France.

The Opinion Way survey reveals a fourth ambiguity, linked to the diversely acceptable nature of dapoxetine prescribed in all parts of the world, combined with the possibility of ordering this substance from unscrupulous suppliers abroad. Differences in marketing authorization between countries lead to a disturbing finding[11]. On the basis of identical or similar clinical

10 Chris McMahon, M.D. Waldinger, Stanley E. Althof, Emmanuele Jannini and François Giuliano are among the most cited authors in this chapter, and are all consultants or lecturers for Menarini and/or other pharmaceutical groups.

11 Ethical, political and economic issues may explain the differences in approvals from one country to another, but the FDA's non-approval decision has remained unchanged for over fifteen years, on the grounds that clinical data remain unsatisfactory.

data, dapoxetine is not considered effective or safe and is not authorized everywhere. These four ambiguities have enabled the Menarini laboratory to implement a two-pronged marketing and communications strategy that is complex and opaque, based on ambiguous discourses and expert figures.

1.3. A textbook case study of a gray-zone communication strategy

1.3.1. *The "scientification" effect and the erasure of the psychological and social dimensions of PE*

The fourfold ambiguity uncovered around scientificity and the legality of prescribing dapoxetine is compounded by a strategy whose every medium aims to convince men of a series of subtly intertwined statements and arguments. Such statements are as follows:

– You suffer from ED if you ejaculate within 7.3 minutes (i.e. the average duration) of sexual intercourse – although the speed of movement is conspicuously not mentioned. This dysfunction is more common than you think and independent of virility and charisma – Napoleon had it.

– The de-dramatization rhetoric is combined with redramatization: PE is painful for you, and your partner. Something must be done about it out of altruism. The TV commercial depicts two matches entwined, and when the larger one ignites, the smaller one sadly bows its head and turns away.

– The partner's deceit is then an incentive to resolve the problem quickly, and chemistry provides modern solutions. Getting more knowledge on your partner's various desires and means to reach orgasm is a no-go. Exogenous and transitory causes that can lead to PE, such as stress or a lack of experience or technique are minor. Even in such cases, a simple, effective and safe therapeutic drug solution can help. All this requires is "talking with your doctor".

This strategy is a roundabout way of getting people to put pressure on their doctor to prescribe a drug to treat their PE. This gray-zone strategy uses media that deceptively exploit ambiguous discursive registers. The website garderlecontrôle.fr and the infographic "*L'éjaculation précoce, parlons-en*!" ("Premature ejaculation, let's talk about it!"), published on October 21, 2014 in various paid and free newspapers, mix semio-discursive codes that link them to different authorships and media genres: information media published by private media or by an authoritative public health institution, publi-information and advertising.

The infographic does not mention the drug's name (Priligy), the name of the molecule or even the pharmaceutical company behind the public relations' company. It can therefore dispense with an accompanying legal mention, which nevertheless seems to impose itself: infomercials. Instead, it simply refers to a website: "Go to www.garderlecontrole.fr to find out more, get advice and let's start a conversation". The website functions more as an advertisement, since it mentions the existence of Priligy by name. These two communication tools are saturated with markers designed to support the scientific nature of the discourse: numerous figures and statistics, which have been self-produced using biased studies; footnotes and definition boxes with almost laughable elements, such as a drawing of a stack of books and, underneath, the Greek translation of the expression "premature ejaculation", under the pretext of etymological precision. Secondly, they relate to the field of scientific popularization with respect of a subtle balance between texts, numerical data and drawings, the profusion of boxes and examples. Finally, the authority of the speech is reinforced by markers embodying the medical field, with two images of silhouettes of doctors, a stethoscope around the neck, at the top left as an exordium, and in place of the peroration at the bottom right. The reading process thus reinforces the authorship of medical prescriptions.

These two communication materials implicitly evoke the situation of a man talking to his doctor about his sexual dissatisfaction and his wish to be prescribed a drug treatment. The man's general practitioner can then refer him to specialists, who can discuss this with him at length in an effort to understand the reality and seriousness of the dysfunction, and its causes. Many general practitioners lack time to talk at length to their patients… The scenario also mentioned the possibility that the general practitioner could comply with his patient's request and prescribe Priligy directly, for reasons of understanding, efficiency and expediency. This option becomes credible to the extent that the request could be expressed forcefully. Then, general practitioners were also the subject of a communication campaign since the marketing authorization for Priligy: sending of leaflets, recruitment of dedicated medical representatives, having stands at various trade fairs, the omnipresence of experts in favor of the prescription of Priligy in numerous mainstream media.

1.3.2. *Ambiguous figures of expertise and experts between science, medicine and marketing of influence*

The success of Menarini's strategy of encouraging and legitimizing Priligy prescriptions is based on its relationships with French experts in sexual health. The laboratory recruits experts with a strong presence in traditional media, but it also maintains their presence through paid spokesperson assignments. These experts possess the legitimacy of their diplomas and their professional practice as caregivers, as well as the legitimacy conferred on them by their peers as elected representatives of France's largest associations for sexual health: the *Fédération française de sexologie et de santé sexuelle* (FF3S), the *Association pour le développement de l'information et de la recherche sur la sexualité* (ADIRS), the *Société francophone de médecine sexuelle* (SFMS) and the *Syndicat national des médecins sexologues* (SNMS). These mandates form the basis of their "right to speak", and therefore their legitimacy to speak out on sexual health issues, beyond the knowledge they have demonstrated through their medical thesis and their membership to the French Order of Physicians.

Menarini's website promotes the opinions of medical experts by featuring quotations and interviews of telegenic experts with medical degrees, which lends weight to the explanations and advice offered. In partnership with FF3S, Menarini also sponsors the Opinion Way survey and the EMOI[12] study, which provide the statistical data to legitimize prescriptions. These "studies" are presented in such a way as to make them appear "scientific", i.e. to endorse or confer a scientific character on them, like a label. In the advertorial page, which takes the form of an infographic, they are cited in the footnotes, in very small type and in black, in stark contrast to the rest of the text. Then, high-profile sexologist Gilbert Bou Jaoudé was one of two speakers present (and paid to do so) at the Menarini press conference that announced the launch of the first national information campaign (on the TV,

12 The EMOI study looked at the impact of PE on psychological well-being and sex life. Presented at a press conference by Menarini, it was carried out in partnership with the French Federation of Sexology and Sexual Health (FF3S). This is the first French observational study investigating PE. It involved 575 patients (and 290 partners) who were selected by 120 sexologists or urologists between October 2013 and April 2014. By commissioning a study, which it then quoted specific passages of to promote the sale of its drug, the laboratory is shaping the reference framework for PE and its medical management in order to protect its interests.

Web and press), and the garderlecontrole.fr website. Titled "*L'éjaculation précoce, il est temps d'en parler*" ("Premature ejaculation, it's time to talk about it"), this press conference seemed to leave the realm of commercial events, and enter the realm of militant events and courageous advocacy. Menarini's intention was to break a sexual taboo with deleterious effects, in line with a major trend in corporate communications towards corporate activism (Dauvergne and LeBaron 2014; Vredenburg et al. 2020). A former president of the SFMS, Dr Bou Jaoudé is also a partner of the website as president and founder of ADIRS. He states, albeit only in some training materials, his contracts with several pharmaceutical groups to serve "as a data presenter and/or chairman at symposia organized by the pharmaceutical industry, consultant, speaker, expert, and investigator"[13].

Similarly, the charles.co "digital clinic", presented as "a platform created and developed by medical experts"[14], is a telemedicine and teleconsultation site that helps to promote the prescription of Priligy. It is complemented by a blog with click-bait articles, a YouTube channel, and profiles on Facebook and X (Twitter). Numerous media (television, press, radio, Web) contribute to the experts'[15] visibility. The scientific director of the digital clinic is, once again, Dr Bou Jaoudé. The "premature ejaculation" section of the clinic's website provides information on "the scientific committee in sexology, a multidisciplinary team made up of medical experts in their fields"[16]. This team includes three doctors in particular: one is the president of the SFMS, the other is the president of the SNMS, and a third teaches at a university, is a founder of the FF3S and the SFMS, is on the editorial board of several sexology journals, is a member of Menarini's advisory board, and also trains medical sales representatives for Menarini. All of these experts state openly in working documents the activities for which they are remunerated by Menarini: consulting, expertise and sponsors of publications.

---

13 In this case, he was referring to a training course organized by the COREVIH Guadeloupe-St Martin-St Barth for people who care for or accompany people living with HIV. See: https://www.corevih971.org/archives/seminaires/article/restitution-de-la-formation-du-31-10-2013-etp-et-sante-sexuelle.

14 See: https:// www.charles.co/approche-medicale/.

15 See: https://www.charles.co/presse/. Examples include *Santé Magazine*, *Le Monde*, *Le Parisien*, *Arte Radio*, *France Culture*, *France Info*, *BFM TV*, *Les Echos*, *Le Mag de la santé*.

16 See: https://www.charles.co/ejaculation-precoce/.

These medical practitioners wear multiple hats and also sometimes have their own social media accounts so they meet the most demanding definitions of marketing influencers (Seccardini and Desmoulins 2023). They publish high-quality, unique, original content on digital social media platforms. They are becoming increasingly professional communicators. For example, they adapt with zeal and creativity to the new platforms, formats and editorial tools. Their accounts may be far removed from the metrics of sports or reality TV stars, but they are well and truly committed to development, which means more subscribers, more likes, more comments and more commercial rewards. They express and lend authority to commercial promises by relaying the results of scientific studies, as well as – more or less explicitly – by drawing on their qualifications and experience as practitioners. Anonymity and pseudoanonymity promote the success of influencer marketing on digital social media applications due to the taboo surrounding ED. In addition, they are sought out by brands (in this case, a pharmaceutical company) to forge partnerships, and also by journalists working for major traditional media (press, TV, radio, podcasts) who are always looking for available, willing and photogenic experts to talk about sexual health – a topic a fortiori conducive to good ratings. Doctors who carry the promise of sexual wellness into the media space derive a substantial part of their income from this activity, while exacerbating "the extension of the commodification of health" (Sedda et al. 2022, p. 24).

On the subject of dapoxetine, experts linked to the Menarini group occupy media, business and academic fields, with editorial jobs at scientific conferences and journals, while being partners with dubious popularization sites. Doctors and scientists not associated with this same industry may not agree with the medical protocol and ethical standards promoted by their telegenic colleagues, but they rarely express themselves in the mainstream media.

Using the metaphor of the ghost, whose presence is obvious and habitual, but discreet and difficult to demonstrate, Sergio Sismondo[17] (2009) explains how private industry interests imperceptibly steer and direct medical research through publications. He analyzes numerous articles in medical journals that report results obtained by research teams who have been funded

17 Sismondo describes corporate science as medical research that is "designed to resemble traditional academic work, but carried out largely to market products" (Sismondo 2009, p. 171).

by pharmaceutical companies, as part of a deliberate strategy to place articles in medical journals, in the same way as product placement in films.

Major links of interest between pharmaceutical companies and doctors may be morally disturbing, but they do not meet the legal definition of a conflict of interest. This is due to the absence of an international, fixed definition of what constitutes a conflict of interest[18]. Laws, regulations and codes of ethics all refer to the possibility of sanctions (such as fines, temporary or permanent removal from the *Conseil de l'Ordre des médecins*, subsequent loss of national license, imprisonment), but these rarely come to pass in reality. Furthermore, relationships of interest, particularly in the medical and pharmaceutical fields, are inevitable and desirable in a capitalist economy as they foster therapeutic innovation.

Moreover, "relationships of interest" do not necessarily mean "conflict of interest", in the sense of a relationship between commercial organizations and scientists that directly undermines the objectivity and integrity of research. The intention to deceive remains to be proven, and, ultimately, it is not our responsibility. Nevertheless, Menarini's marketing and communications strategy relies very effectively on experts who are as distinguished as they are well-connected, helping to establish PE as a health problem, and to convince men to request a prescription of Priligy. The recruitment of scientists and practitioners by the pharmaceutical industry has already been identified by researchers in agnotology[19] as a systematic strategy in research driven by commercial interests.

1.4. Conclusion

The problematic links between experts and companies combine with the lack of critical perspective of journalists and columnists on science, even those specialized in science popularization. It points as well to our limited capacity to distinguish from a conceptual and practical point of view new forms of perversion of research, expertise and scientific popularization.

18 In France, see, for example, Article 2 of the law of October 11, 2013 on transparency in public life, which defines a "conflict of interest" for the first time; "the "Bertrand Law" of December 29, 2011, known as the "anti-gift, ethics and transparency act" on the reinforcement of the safety of medicines and health products; and transparence.gouv.

19 For an introduction to the study of ignorance, see, for example, Proctor (2008), Oreskes and Conway (2010), Fernández Pinto (2017).

Considered as a whole, PE, the promotion of dapoxetine and its prescription seem to provide a paradigmatic case of ambiguity: the coexistence of different clinical definitions and names reflects a semantic ambiguity that makes it difficult to interpret results. The multifactorial nature of PE, and the fact that dapoxetine's mechanism of action remains unexplained, reflect forms of etiological and therapeutic ambiguity. Secondly, dapoxetine prescription enjoys a dual status as both an *acceptable* and *unacceptable* medical practice. The over-representation of studies funded or produced by scientists closely linked to pharmaceutical companies challenges our way of categorizing acceptable and unacceptable science, research *driven* by commercial and industrial interests and research *corrupted* by them. On the other hand, this fourfold ambiguity, which to a large extent reflects the lack of medical data, is clearly problematic when accompanied by gray-zone communication strategy.

Darkness stems from media that exploit ambiguous, and therefore misleading, discursive registers (private information media/advertising websites, infographics emanating from a public health institution/ infomercial), and the recruitment of questionable high-profile expert figures. This study suffers from the limitations inherent in surveys of strategies for gray-zone communication (Dulek and Campbell 2015; Carayol et al. 2019; Desmoulins 2019). We were not able to observe what went on in the offices of general practitioners who received Menarini medical visitors, nor were we able to interview the doctors involved in the legitimization system uncovered. We also have no knowledge of the precise timing of the media coverage of all the materials used in this communication campaign, its coordination procedures and actual costs, or how successful it was in increasing prescriptions of Priligy/dapoxetine[20]. It would obviously be helpful to conduct interviews with men taking Priligy, and with their partners, in order to understand their sexual health pathways, as well as their representation and experiences in relation to Priligy and other treatments or practices linked to sexual wellbeing. However, this research has already highlighted the effectiveness of a pharmaceutical company's communication strategy and media for promoting a drug in a partially masked way, based on a combination of methodological bias and the representativeness of studies,

20 One of the very few incriminating articles published on November 26, 2013 by Alice Maruani on the *Nouvel Observateur* website goes into more detail about this campaign. See: https://www.nouvelobs.com/societe/20131126.OBS7003/ejaculation-precoce-la-pub-cachee-derriere-la-campagne-choc.html.

and using highly credible "in-house experts" and thus able to legitimize and encourage the prescription of a controversial drug.

1.5. References

Althof, S.E., McMahon, C.G., Waldinger, M.D., Serefoglu, E.C., Shindel, A.W., Adaikan, P.G., Becher, E., Dean, J., Giuliano, F., Hellstrom, W.J. et al. (2014). An update of the International Society of Sexual Medicine's guidelines for the diagnosis and treatment of premature ejaculation (PE). *Sexual Medicine*, 2(2), 60–90. doi: 10.1002/sm2.28.

Carayol, V., Lépine, V., Morillon, L. (eds) (2019). *Le côté obscur de la communication des organisations*. Org&Co, Maison des Sciences de l'Homme d'Aquitaine, Pessac.

Chapman, P.S. and Beltramini, R.F. (2000). Infomercials revisited: Perspectives of advertising professionals. *Journal of Advertising Research*, 40, 24–31.

Clément, P., Laurin, M., Compagnie, S., Facchinetti, P., Bernabé, J., Alexandre, L., Giuliano, F. (2012). Effect of dapoxetine on ejaculatory performance and related brain neuronal activity in rapid ejaculator rats. *The Journal of Sexual Medicine*, 9(10), 2562–2573.

Dauvergne, P. and LeBaron, G. (2014). *Protest Inc: The Corporatization of Activism*. Polity, Cambridge.

Debray, S. (2022a). Le problème de la démarcation : une (nouvelle) définition de la pseudoscience. *Revue des Questions Scientifiques*, 3–4, 301–352.

Debray, S. (2022b). Questions médicales controversées, déclarations de consensus et participation du public : le cas des conférences de consensus du National Institute of Health. *Dialogue: Canadian Philosophical Review / Revue canadienne de philosophie*, 61(1), 55–81.

Desmoulins, L. (2017). Pédagogie et dilemmes de l'enseignement de l'éthique du lobbying. *Communication & Professionnalisation*, 5, 122–144.

Desmoulins, L. (2019). Faire et contrefaire des discours scientifiques : une forme "normale" de communication stratégique ? In *Le "côté obscur" de la communication des organisations*, Carayol, V., Lépine, V., Morillon, L. (eds). Org&Co, Maison des Sciences de l'Homme d'Aquitaine, Pessac.

Dulek, R.E. and Campbell, K.S. (2015). On the dark side of strategic communication. *International Journal of Business Communication*, 52, 122–142.

Fernández Pinto, M. (2017). To know or better not to: Agnotology and the social construction of ignorance in commercially driven research. *Science & Technology Studies*, 30, 53–72.

Feys, F. (ed.) (2015). Dapoxetine for premature ejaculation: A harmful placebo? PhD Thesis, Université de Bruxelles, Brussels.

Jannini, E.A., Eardley, I., Sand, M., and Hackett, G. (2010). Controversies in sexual medicine: Clinical and basic science research in sexual medicine must rely, in part, on pharmaceutical funding? *The Journal of Sexual Medicine*, 7(7), 2331–2337.

McMahon, C.G. (2012). Dapoxetine: A new option in the medical management of premature ejaculation. *Therapeutic Advances in Urology*, 4, 233–251.

Oreskes, N. and Conway, E.M. (2010). *Merchants of Doubt: How a Handful of Scientists Obscured the Truth on Issues from Tobacco Smoke to Global Warming*. Bloomsbury Publishing, New York.

Prescrire (2009). Dapoxétine (Priligy°). Éjaculation prématurée, le jeu n'en vaut pas la chandelle. *Prescrire*, 29(313), 811–814.

Prescrire (2013). Éjaculation précoce : pas de dapoxétine (Priligy°) [Online]. Available at: https://prescrire.org/fr/3/31/48533/0/NewsDetails.aspx.

Prescrire (2021). Pour mieux soigner, des médicaments à écarter : bilan 2022. *Prescrire*, 41(458), 935–947.

Proctor, R.N. (2008). Agnotology: A missing term to describe the cultural production of ignorance (and its study). In *Agnotology: The Making and Unmaking of Ignorance*, Proctor, R.N. and Schiebinger, L. (eds). Stanford University Press, Stanford.

Sangkum, P., Badr, R., Serefoglu, E.C., Hellstrom, W.J.G. (2013). Dapoxetine and the treatment of premature ejaculation. *Translational Andrology and Urology*, 2, 301–311.

Seccardini, G., and Desmoulins, L. (2023). Flawed public diplomacy: When Croatia Instagram Riviera narrative destination branding ignores dark tourism amateurs. *Journal of Communication Management*, 27(2), 277–292. doi: 10.1108/JCOM-04-2022-0039.

Sedda, P., Botero, N., Orellana, M.H. (2022). Influenceurs et influenceuses santé : les récits et les savoirs du corps sur les réseaux sociaux. *Études de communication. Langages, information, médiations*, 58, 7–24.

Sismondo, S. (2009). Ghosts in the machine: Publication planning in the medical sciences. *Social Studies of Science*, 39(2), 171–198.

Vredenburg, J., Kapitan, S., Spry, A., Kemper, J.A. (2020). Brands taking a stand: Authentic brand activism or woke washing? *Journal of Public Policy & Marketing*, 39, 444–460.

Waldinger, M.D. (2002). The neurobiological approach to premature ejaculation. *The Journal of Urology*, 168(6), 2359–2367.

Waldinger, M.D. and Schweitzer, D.H. (2008). Premature ejaculation and pharmaceutical company-based medicine: The dapoxetine case. *The Journal of Sexual Medicine*, 5, 966–997.

2

Battle of Expertise and Experts in the Media: The Case of Glyphosate (2000–2020)

2.1. Introduction

In 1951, Auguste Detœuf wrote in his book, *Propos de O.-L. Barenton, confiseur*, "[n]obody believes the experts, but everybody listens to them". Whether it is mad cow disease (Granjou 2009), asbestos (Henry 2007) or contaminated blood (Marchetti 2010), expert reports and the experts who bring them into the public arena play a fundamental role in the construction of public health problems in the media. The potential carcinogenicity of Monsanto's flagship herbicide, glyphosate, is no exception. The endurance of glyphosate in the French media is due to numerous expert reports and the various media discourses that punctuate it. Indeed, while the ways in which scientific sources are used by the media is well documented in the context of public health issues (Bouillon 2012), this literature remains relatively insufficient on the topic of pesticides. In this respect, our contribution provides an excellent entry point to the literature on this topic, specifically to the mechanisms of (de)legitimization and appropriation of expertise at work by the journalists who bring it into the media arena, as well as their driving motivations.

So, how do experts impose themselves on the media, and how do journalists seek to impose certain types of expertise?

Chapter written by Baptiste SCHUMMER.

The title of this chapter, which delves into a particularly heuristic aspect of a set of more global reflections regarding the media coverage of glyphosate in France (Schummer 2022), draws on "battles" as a common theme. The first part will deal chronologically with the battles of expertise in the media – i.e. the ways in which the various expert reports (by both academic and lay experts) on this biocide (Masse 2012) were publicized and placed on the journalistic agenda between 2000 and 2019 by media, journalistic, economic, scientific, activist and legal players. The second part will address the ways in which journalists appropriate these forms of expertise to act as experts in media battles. We will focus on January 2019, when an episode of *Envoyé spécial*[1] aired, called "*Glyphosate : comment s'en sortir* ?" (Glyphosate: How do we cope?). An X (Twitter) battle then ensued between the "anti" and "pro" glyphosate camps of French journalism. We will study this moment of crystallization of conflicts over the molecule's (non) dangerousness between journalists from both camps, to identify the strategies and instrumentalization of the various expert opinions in light of the media battles waged by journalists on social networks and within their respective media.

In terms of research methodology, this work is based on two corpora: the first corpus was compiled from Europresse articles containing the words "glyphosate" or "Roundup" in the five most widely circulated titles in the French general press (*Le Figaro*, *Le Monde*, *Le Parisien/Aujourd'hui en France, La Croix*, *Libération*); the second was compiled by bringing together all audiovisual archival material between 2000 and 2020 available from the *Institut national audiovisuel* (INA). After reconstructing the two "networks of operators" (Hilgartner 1988) in the media coverage of glyphosate, we conducted 30 interviews with members of the two respective "coalitions of circumstance" that were (re)formed around this problematic issue – a total of nine journalists, five members of agricultural unions, four academics, four popular science communicators, four lobbyists, two activists and two Bayer/Monsanto executives.

2.2. Battles of expertise in the media

The enduring media fascination with glyphosate – the active ingredient in Monsanto's flagship weedkiller, Roundup – has been marked by battles

1 "*Envoyé Spécial*" is a popular French investigative news show. For example, this episode has been watched by 3 million viewers.

between experts who have questioned (repeatedly) its potential danger to human health. First marketed in 1975, this "total herbicide" has been used on a massive scale since the late 1990s, when the company launched a GMO range of glyphosate-tolerant NK603 maize called "Roundup Ready". While the potential danger of Roundup did not attract much media attention until 2011 (section 2.2.1), an initial study into Roundup's carcinogenicity publicized its carcinogenic risk to humans between 2012 and 2014 (section 2.2.2). From 2015 onwards, glyphosate itself became the subject of a veritable "social controversy with a scientific theme" (Charaudeau 2014) (section 2.2.3), as shown in Figure 2.1.

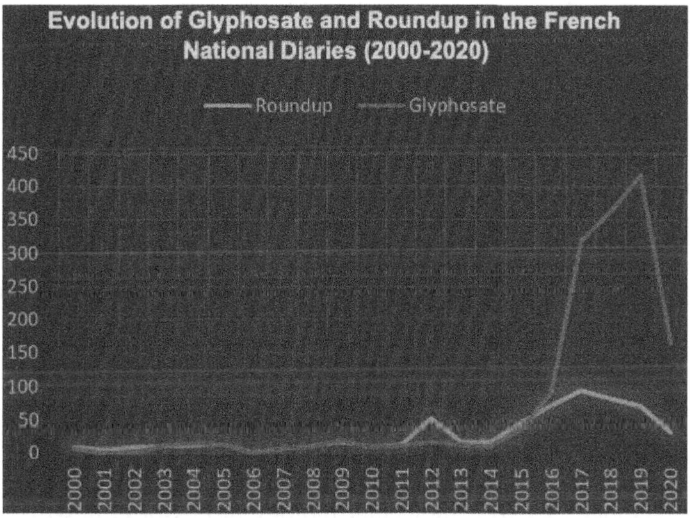

Figure 2.1. *Evolution of glyphosate and Roundup in the French National Diaries. For a color version of this figure, see www.iste.co.uk/corroy/health.zip*

2.2.1. *Lay experts versus GMOs (2000–2011)*

In Figure 2.1, which lists articles about Roundup and glyphosate in the five major publications of the French daily press, the absence of media interest in the issue is particularly striking between 2000 and 2011. What is more, the way journalists chose to frame the issue at the time had nothing to do with the pesticide's potential threat to health, which would later feature heavily in the French media. During the first decade of the 2000s, Roundup was a symbol in the fight against GMOs, at a time when the media spotlight was on campaigns to uproot GMO cornfields, notably embodied by José Bové and the *Faucheurs volontaires d'OGM* movement. In the handful of articles that mention Roundup, it is not the main subject, but merely a secondary element in an anti-Monsanto framing, which is not based on any expertise that highlights its potential dangerousness.

> At the time, in the 2000s, there were hardly any studies, just a sense of concern among activists that was almost intuitive, let's say instinctive. (Frédéric, science journalist in the "*Planète*" section of *Le Monde*, 12/01/2021)

These comments show that while the issue of Roundup had only marginal presence in French newspapers during this time, the media presented the pesticide as a contextual element in a journalistic narrative about the struggle of anti-globalization activists against a phytosanitary industry whose practices were considered dubious. We can point to the documentary *Le Monde selon Monsanto* – broadcast several times on *Arte* and directed by investigative journalist Marie-Monique Robin – as a good example of this hegemonic framing. At the time, the potential carcinogenicity of the product was not on the media agenda. It was in September 2012, at the start of what would later be dubbed the "Séralini affair", that the French media began framing Roundup as a health threat.

2.2.2. *An outcry against Roundup! The Séralini affair: putting a health threat on the media agenda (2012–2014)*

On September 19, 2012, molecular biology professor Gilles-Éric Séralini published a scientific article, which he later retracted, on the toxicity of Roundup and Monsanto's GMO corn NK603. This was the first step that led to the framing of Roundup as a health threat to the general public. This unconventional media staging was achieved by a communications agency and financed by supermarket chains keen to invest in the lucrative GMO-free market. The resulting violation of the principle of the information embargo, specific to the operating principles of scientific journalism (Allard-Huver 2020), gave Roundup access to certain media outlets through a new framing of GMOs as receptacles for the potentially dangerous substances contained in the herbicide (including glyphosate), affecting food and thus extending the health risk to all French people. The consequences of Séralini's article in media were considerable, as illustrated by the front page of *Le Nouvel Observateur* on September 20, 2012 (Figure 2.2). Following this "media coup"

(Champagne 2011), Séralini became the leading expert in the media on Roundup, as well as the carcinogenicity of pesticides in general. This was the first case of highly publicized academic expertise –though the article was subsequently invalidated – that placed the herbicide in the dock. While the “Séralini affair” led to a spike in the mentions of “Roundup” in the French national press in 2012 (see Figure 2.1), this publicity remained moderate compared to the publicity surrounding its active molecule, glyphosate, three years later.

Figure 2.2. *Front page of* Nouvel Observateur, *September 20, 2012. For a color version of this figure, see www.iste.co.uk/corroy/health.zip*

2.2.3. *From Roundup to glyphosate: expertise and counter-expertise (2015–2018)*

In March 2015, the International Agency for Research on Cancer (IARC), a branch of the World Health Organization (WHO), published a report that confirmed the probable carcinogenicity of glyphosate to human health. Later, in November 2015, the European Food Safety Authority (EFSA), Europe’s main health agency, refuted this claim. This marked the beginning of a long battle between expert and counter-expert opinions and their two opposing conceptions of science: on the one hand, fundamental research, and, on the other, so-called regulatory research, or risk assessment. This conflict between the IARC’s fundamental research and EFSA’s regulatory toxicology sparked the war of academic expertise that was raging around glyphosate. This epistemological struggle rested on three pillars (Boullier 2021):

– risk or hazard assessment;

– the weight of epidemiological data;

– the number of studies produced using industry data.

The first pillar, and the most fundamental one, refers to the adage, "the dose makes the poison", credited to Paracelsus as the founder of modern toxicology. Regulatory toxicology, as embodied by EFSA, focuses on risk, i.e. the danger of the product multiplied by the level of exposure (or dose). By contrast, the IARC is only concerned with calculating the intrinsic danger of the product, without taking into account the levels of exposure to which populations may be exposed. This dominant Paracelsian paradigm is criticized by proponents of a fundamental science operating on the principle of peer review, like the IARC, who cite the example of endocrine disruptors (such as bisphenol A) that can have adverse long-term effects on human health at very low levels of exposure.

This first epistemological divergence leads us to a second area of scientific disagreement, which concerns the temporality of the studies used to compile the meta-analyses of each of the two organizations. While the IARC places great emphasis on long-term epidemiological studies, these data only play a marginal role in EFSA's results (Jouzel 2019). This discordance in terms of temporality is central, as it pits regulatory agencies responsible for ruling on the release of a potentially dangerous product in the short term against other scientific bodies that take into account the entire scientific literature to assess its potential repercussions over the long term.

This divide in the scientific literature taken into account in the two agencies' calculations brings us to our third and final difference between the two scientific systems. Whereas the IARC does not take industrial studies into account in its calculations, EFSA also relies on data supplied by agrochemical companies, making its conclusions partly dependent on corporate funding (Krimsky 2013). This relative porosity between the spheres of production and regulatory assessment is central, especially when we are aware of the ghostwriting practices mobilized by Monsanto, which were revealed to the general public in the "*Planète*" section of *Le Monde* by journalists Stéphane Foucart and Stéphane Horel as part of the "Monsanto Papers" published in October 2017.

While these two epistemic communities, whose results diverge according to opposing conceptions of scientificity and antagonistic working habits, struggle for a monopoly on defining the (non)dangerousness of glyphosate rages in the media (Meyer and Molyneux-Modgson 2011), these two types of expertise can be instrumentalized by journalists, who see them as sources of (de)legitimization. Having seen how the words of experts take over the media, it remains to be seen how journalists seize on expertise to wage their media battles.

2.3. Experts in media battles

In order to understand the ways in which the different registers of expertise are appropriated by journalists involved in the public controversy surrounding glyphosate, we propose to focus on the most fundamental event in the media coverage of glyphosate in France. An episode of *Envoyé spécial* devoted to glyphosate on France 2 marked the peak of French public interest in the glyphosate issue, beating by a narrow margin the revelation of the "Monsanto Papers", which nevertheless enjoyed worldwide renown, as illustrated in Figure 2.3.

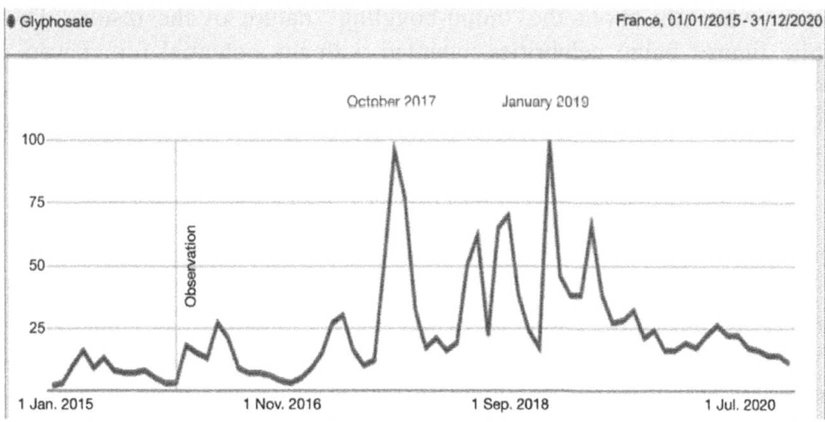

Figure 2.3. *Glyphosate on Google Trends. For a color version of this figure, see www.iste.co.uk/corroy/health.zip*

For the purposes of this chapter, our interest in this program is less about its large-scale reach (it was viewed nearly 3 million times), but instead because of the quality of the spotlight it shines on the (di)visions of the registers of expertise mobilized by the journalists involved in the informational battles they waged over the herbicide's (non)harmlessness.

2.3.1. *Lay expertise as anti-glyphosate evidence*

This episode of *Envoyé spécial* opens with Élise Lucet, the show's iconic presenter, as she strolls past the market stands in Marly-le-Roi, a commune in the Yvelines department. She asks people for their opinions on glyphosate, and then asks them to take a "glyphotest", a urine test that is analyzed by the BioCheck laboratory to measure the levels of glyphosate in their bodies. This public "urine war" echoes the campaign strategy developed by the association *Campagne glyphosate*, heir to the aforementioned *Faucheurs Volontaires* movement, whose activists call themselves "involuntary glyphosate pissers" (Allard-Huver 2021). Although she stops short of ruling definitively on the question of glyphosate's carcinogenicity, Lucet nevertheless doubles down on the opinion of "a WHO agency" (the IARC) in the face of "differing opinions". This archetypal example of lay expertise involving "ordinary" people, is backed up here by another media device featuring the astonished reactions of media personalities such as Julie Gayet, Jamel Debbouze, Lilian Thuram and Kevin Mayer, who talk about the "mind-boggling" nature of the results. These public figures being celebrities, coupled with the potential for viewers to connect with ordinary people, contributes to the effectiveness of a media device that places lay expertise in the service of an anti-glyphosate argument.

Other forms of lay expertise are also present in the show. The case of Théo Grataloup, an 11-year-old child who is said to have been intoxicated in utero when his mother weeded her riding school using Glyper, an off-brand version of Monsanto's Roundup, while she was pregnant, is emblematic of how valuable a potential victim's "experiential expertise" (Borkman 1976) can be for anti-glyphosate journalists. Grataloup suffers from a congenital anomaly that has caused his respiratory and digestive systems to communicate. Both he and his mother blame his disability on the glyphosate molecule marketed by Monsanto. In the words of Sabine Grataloup, this mobilization of lay expertise thus stands up in opposition to the scientific expertise of health agencies, taken up by pro-glyphosate journalists, as well as public authorities:

> We're trying to make them aware [...]. That it's not a battle of experts or choosing a side. We're not choosing sides. We're a family with a suffering child.

2.3.2. *Academic expertise as the sinews of journalistic warfare*

Indeed, beyond the marginal role that lay experts are struggling to play, it is academic expertise that constitutes the focal point of the public controversy pitting pro- and anti-glyphosate journalists against each other. Before detailing the way in which members of both camps (de)legitimize certain scholarly expertise in ways similar to those described in Part 1, we need to model the two coalitions of circumstance that formed in the wake of the broadcast (Table 2.1).

Position statements / Nature	Pro-glyphosate	Anti-glyphosate
Journalists	Aline (*L'Opinion*) Valérie (*Le Point*) Mac Lesggy (M6)	Frédéric (*Le Monde*) Angélique (*Le Monde*) Aurélien (France 2)
Experts	Applied research EFSA AFIS and no fake science	Fundamental research IARC Criigen
Mobilization actors	FNSEA Monsanto FranceAgriTwittos	*Confédération paysanne* *Générations Futures* *Justice Pesticides*
Political actors	French Ministry of Agriculture Stéphane Travert Didier Guillaume	French Ministry of Ecology Ségolène Royal Nicolas Hulot
Economic actors	Liberal think-tanks (Institut Sapiens) Pesticide lobbies (UIPP)	GMO-free supermarket chains Organic farming companies (FNAB)
Legal actors	Lawyers for Bayer/Monsanto	Environmental lawyers

Table 2.1. *Actors and their stances*

On the one hand, members of the anti-glyphosate group (investigative journalists at *Le Monde*, France 2, supporters of fundamental and public research, associations of pesticide victims, environmentalist politicians, organic farming companies and lawyers specializing in environmental issues) share a common scepticism towards the expertise promoted by health agencies. This was confirmed by the interview with Stéphane Foucart, one of the two *Le Monde* journalists who revealed the "Monsanto Papers" to the French public, in which he meticulously deciphered the conflicts of interest between Monsanto and certain scientists, which translate into techniques for manipulating expertise by the phytosanitary firm. Similarly, the presence of Séralini, not "as a scientific guarantor", but as an "essential protagonist of the story of the Monsanto Papers" as argued by Manon, a journalist at *Envoyé spécial*, is indicative of the epistemic distrust that anti-glyphosate journalists harbor with regard to the modes of production of institutionally regulated expertise. Thus, one of the methods of administering proof used by anti-glyphosate journalists consists of investigating the biases produced by certain experimental protocols concluding that glyphosate is safe, and consequently delegitimizing the arguments put forward by supporters of the re-registration of the molecule (economic and/or agricultural journalists, regulatory expertise, unions and politicians supporting intensive agriculture, liberal lobbies and think tanks, the phytosanitary industry and their legal representatives).

In this model, the "pro-glyphosate" journalists retaliate with salvoes of now deleted X's (Tweets), which are spontaneous and immediate manifestations of their representations of the world. As such, they criticize the supposedly activist and scientific nature of the sources used by the *Envoyé spécial* journalists:

> This Élise Lucet show is a web of insinuations and lies. How can you say that Monsanto corrupted hundreds of researchers without any proof!!! (Aline, January 17, 2019)

The media battles between pro- and anti-glyphosate journalists are also raging over the scholarly expertise expressed in this episode of *Envoyé spécial*, which serves as an alternative to the opinions of health agencies. In addition to Séralini's much-criticized appearance on the program, other fundamental research studies are the subject of debate. This is particularly true of the final sequence on Sri Lanka, the first country in the world to issue a total ban on glyphosate in 2015 as a precautionary measure. This political decision was scientifically based on the aforementioned IARC opinion, as well as the work of Channa Jayasumana, a scientist who was interviewed on the show and supposedly has evidence of a correlation between glyphosate and a kidney disease affecting the national population. This sparked a new epistemic controversy between pro- and anti-glyphosate journalists regarding the scientific nature of this evidence and expertise, and on which the editors of *Envoyé spécial* refused to comment. According to an article published by *CheckNews*, the fact-checking arm of the *Libération* newspaper, dated January 23, 2019:

> By refusing, by choice, to enter into the fundamental debate on the scientific evidence of the danger of glyphosate, but by giving the floor to complainants and researchers Gilles-Éric Séralini and Channa Jayasumana, France 2 is nonetheless open to criticism for its scientific handling of the case.

More than these attempts to (de)legitimize these two expert reports aimed at demonstrating the toxicity of glyphosate, it is undoubtedly the legal victory of Dewayne Johnson – an American gardener suffering from terminal cancer who used glyphosate-based herbicides between 2012 and 2015 – against Monsanto, which best illustrates these journalistic oppositions that mobilize different expert registers. In August 2018, Monsanto was ordered to pay him $289 million in damage after a jury in San Francisco found Ranger Pro (composed of 41% glyphosate) to be a major cause of his non-Hodgkin's lymphoma. In reaction to the presence of Dewayne Johnson in the show, pro-glyphosate journalists used the same tactic for compiling evidence, by enlisting regulatory toxicology and the Paracelsian axiom according to which "the dose makes the poison", on which the majority of health agencies rely to delegitimize opposing legal-scientific expertise. The exploitation of this dominant paradigm of scholarly toxicological expertise in the context of the Dewayne Johnson trial constitutes a valuable resource for pro-glyphosate journalists:

> This man was literally bathed in the product. (Valérie, January 23, 2019)

Indeed, journalists share common conceptions of expertise with fellow members of their coalition of circumstance, but it is the ways in which they operate multiple registers of expertise that differentiate them. While anti-glyphosate journalists investigate and criticize the biases of institutionally regulated expertise, pro-glyphosate journalists take on the role of relaying the expertise of health agencies, which they regard as scientifically legitimate. More than (di)visions of the practice of the profession, these (di)visions of expertise above all reveal the (di)visions of the world that oppose journalists from both camps.

2.3.3. *Expertise as a Trojan horse for ideology*

> Glyphosate divides the farming world. In the fields, there are those who work with it, and then there are those who work without it. We've tried to bring these two seemingly irreconcilable worlds together.

These are the words spoken by Lucet at the beginning of the first part of the program, called "Glypho or not glypho?". This section contrasts the production methods used by Vincent, a pro-glyphosate farmer, with those used by organic farmer Olivier. This sharing of experience and expertise between these two professionals serves as a model of the controversy between its two extremes. Under the guise of specific technical expertise, the two farmers clash over ideological (di)visions that function in homology with those of the coalitions of circumstance to which they belong and those of their standard-bearer journalists.

If, by definition, the expert is the one with the knowledge, they are also the one whom journalists choose to trust or not. Depending on the type/s of expertise they recognize as legitimate, pro- and anti-glyphosate journalists support particular modes of knowledge production that condition political decision-making on the (non-)re-registration of glyphosate, and consequently advocate certain modes of agricultural and economic production that are in line with their representations of the world. The scholarly registers used by journalists in their media battles over the (non)dangerousness of glyphosate therefore resonate with the political and even ideological (di)visions that determine the choice of publicized expert reports, criteria that are far more subjective than the alleged scientificity they claim to uphold. More than discursive resources, expert reports act as screens that conceal the underlying political motivations, thus seemingly meeting the professional standard of excellence of journalistic distancing vis-à-vis of and from politics (Kaciaf 2014). However, we can separate these political motivations from the rhetorical strategies different actors employ (see Table 2.2).

The words of experts function as a pool that journalists can draw from according to their particular social positions and ideological stances, which is why they accuse one another of cherry picking, i.e. selecting the statements that suit them best in order to discredit the "junk science" perpetuated by members of the other camp. The cornerstone of the opposition between journalists lies in their relationship with the established order, embodied by the institutions labeled as (il)legitimate according to their positioning. Pro-glyphosate journalists relay the opinions of health agencies, which they view as epistemic authorities that are trustworthy, while anti-glyphosate journalists investigate the dysfunctional dynamics of these institutions, focusing in particular on their links to phytosanitary companies, such as Monsanto. This has earned pro-glyphosate journalists the nickname "merchants of doubt" (Oresken and Conway 2010). Anti-glyphosate journalists ridicule pro-glyphosate journalists as "guardians of reason" (Foucart et al. 2020), accusing them of exploiting rationality to sow seeds of doubt about the (non)danger of glyphosate and its re-registration. Conversely, pro-glyphosate journalists criticize their opponents for being ideologues who would exploit expertise for the sake of their activism, calling them "watermelons", i.e. promoting anti-capitalist (red) ideas under the guise of ecological (green) garb.

Rhetorical positions	**Pro-glyphosate journalists**	**Anti-glyphosate journalists**
Arguments mobilized	Facts and figures The difference between risk and danger "The dose makes the poison"	Emotions, care Distrust of industrial studies Precautionary principle
Strategies used to (dis)qualify the opponent: **"You are…"** **"You convey…"** **"You practice…"**	Merchants of doubt Phytosanitary lobbyists Guardians of reason Junk science Cherry picking	Merchants of fear Organic industry lobbyists Militants (watermelons) Junk science Cherry picking
"You practice…" **"You are…"**	Journalism of reverence Representatives of power	Preference journalists Ideologists
"You are at the service of…"	Knowledgeable Dominant	Believers Dominated

Table 2.2. *Arguments used*

Ultimately, the objective veneer provided by expertise is journalistically very useful. It serves a cosmetic function to conceal normative assumptions about glyphosate, the French agricultural system, as well as more general political games. Above all, it is the malleable nature of expertise that explains its omnipresence in media battles over socio-technical controversies, whose stakes go beyond the strictly scientific framework, such as the one that took glyphosate as its subject. This plasticity of expertise makes it a formidable rhetorical weapon, at the heart of the digital battles being waged by journalists on both sides, who have themselves become experts in turn.

2.4. Conclusion

While we began this chapter by showing how the words of experts had divided and dominated the processing of information relating to the (non) harmfulness of glyphosate throughout its time in the French media, we moved to focus on the fact that the expertise constituted arsenals particularly prized by the journalists most engaged in the informational battles that punctuate the media chronology of this socio-technical controversy. However, if we were able to show that the instrumentalization of expertise by journalists from both sides assigned it the function of a Trojan horse of ideologies, it is nevertheless necessary to differentiate the aims that it pursues depending on the position of its agents. Thus, anti-glyphosate journalists use alternative expertise as a counter to official expertise and its biases in order to challenge the established order, which they consider to be both unjust and failing, and to defend the "journalism of reverence" of pro-glyphosate journalists, or "representatives of power", who seek to preserve the dominant political, economic and social order. Conversely, supporters of glyphosate, who persistently take the side of expertise produced by epistemic authorities, despite the fact that these institutions have been damaged considerably by the revelations of their colleagues, constitute an important metajournalistic paradox. Is the role of journalists in a democracy to act as sounding boards for official discourse through a register of "this goes without saying"? Or, on the contrary, should it bring out other points of view that compete with institutional speech in the name of pluralism, polyphony and equality of discourse? Applying this thorny question to scientific subjects is a particularly perilous exercise, because it is clear that not all knowledge on the matter is equal, as illustrated by media jurisprudence regarding climate skepticism:

> The principle of good journalism is to treat both sides equally. In theory, you support the weak, the oppressed, the dominated more than the official word which has plenty of other channels to express itself. I get sad when I see colleagues hide behind a theory that is supposed to be well-intentioned, by giving more weight to counter-powers than to the establishment in their work. That's all well and good, but because of this, there was a time when Claude Allègre had a bigger platform than climate scientists to talk about the climate. […] We cannot put them on an equal footing, it isn't possible, because we make viewers believe that there are two sides which have the same recognized scientific competence on the subject. But this isn't true! For me, this is professional misconduct. (Pierre-André, science journalist at *Libération*, January 27, 2021)

Nevertheless, in the case of glyphosate, given the clear interference of the phytosanitary companies (namely Monsanto) in the expert production processes used by pro-glyphosate journalists, the latter's stance once again raises the age-old question of journalism's role as a counterweight in France:

> The journalist cannot be "with" power without denying themselves. But one is not always aware of being "with" power. Being "with" means, for example, no longer believing that you must verify a figure from a representative of power and to cross-check it with other sources; or pouting at a given demonstration, perhaps ironizing, but without bringing reality, a fact, an "experience", a study, an "otherness" that makes it possible to distance oneself from the official point of view. (Muhlmann 2006)

2.5. References

Allard-Huver, F. (2020). Gilles-Éric Séralini ou la transgression des médiations "traditionnelles" du savoir ? *Revue française des sciences de l'information et de la communication*, 20.

Allard-Huver, F. (2021). Glyphosate, la "guerre des urines" a bien eu lieu. *Les Enjeux de l'information et de la communication*, 22(3B), 11–24.

Borkman, T. (1976). Experiential knowledge: A new concept for the analysis of self-help groups. *Social Service Review*, 50(3), 445–456.

Bouillon, J.L. (2012). L'expertise scientifique en société : regards communicationnels. *Hermès, La Revue*, 64, 14–21.

Boullier, H. (2021). Derrière le spectre des "conflits d'intérêts" généralisés. Les agences face aux défis de l'évaluation réglementaire de produits. *Natures Sciences Sociétés*, 29(1), 103–108.

Champagne, P. (2011). Le coup médiatique. Les journalistes font-ils l'événement ? *Sociétés & Représentations*, 32, 25–43.

Charaudeau, P. (ed.) (2014). La situation de communication comme fondatrice d'un genre : la controverse. In *Genres & textes. Déterminations, évolutions, confrontations. Études offertes à Jean-Michel Adam*. Presses universitaires de Lyon, Lyon.

Foucart, S., Horel, S., Laurens, S. (2020). *Les gardiens de la raison. Enquête sur la désinformation scientifique*. La Découverte, Paris.

Granjou, C. (2009). Entre santé animale et santé publique, un problème "discret". La carrière de la tremblante ovine. *Comment se construisent les problèmes de santé publique*. La Découverte, Paris.

Henry, E. (2007). *Amiante : un scandale improbable, sociologie d'un problème public*. Presses Universitaires de Rennes, Rennes.

Hilgartner, S. and Bosk, C.L. (1988). The rise and fall of social problems: A public arenas model. *American Journal of Sociology*, 94(1), 53–78.

Jouzel, J.N. (2019). *Pesticides : comment ignorer ce que l'on sait*. Presses de Sciences Po, Paris.

Kaciaf, N. (2014). Communication politique et distanciation journalistique. Les transformations contemporaines des pages Politique de la presse écrite française. *Savoir/Agir*, 28, 13–18.

Krimsky, S. (2013). Do financial conflicts of interest bias research? *Science, Technology, & Human Values*, 38(4), 566–587.

Marchetti, D. (2010). *Quand la santé devient médiatique. Les logiques de production de l'information dans la presse*. Presses universitaires de Grenoble, Grenoble.

Masse, R. (2012). Expertises éthiques savantes et profanes en santé publique : défis et enjeux pour une éthique de la discussion. *Santé Publique*, 24(1), 49–61.

Meyer, M. and Molyneux-Modgson, S. (2011). Communautés épistémiques : une notion utile pour théoriser les collectifs en sciences ? *Terrains & travaux*, 18, 141–154.

Muhlmann, G. (2006). Le gros mot de contre-pouvoir. *Pouvoirs*, 119(4), 55–70.

Oreskes, N. and Conway, E (2010). *Merchants of Doubt: How a Handful of Scientists Obscured the Truth on Issues from Tobacco Smoke to Global Warming*. Bloomsbury Press, New York.

Schummer, B. (2022). Le glyphosate et les journalistes en France. La construction sociale d'un problème public médiatisé (2000–2020). *Sur le journalisme, About journalism*, 11(2), 44–61.

3

The Influence of Opinion Leaders on Health Shows: *L'Amour en Questions* (1994–1998)

3.1. Introduction

Since the beginning of public television, experts have been consulted on health programs (Pierre 2012, p. 82), representing the strong ties between the media and professionals. While historical context is necessary to properly understand the issues surrounding the place of experts on TV, it also allows us to explore the figure of the "opinion leader", which is crucial for understanding expert influence. In light of the increasing use of experts on health television shows, this chapter will reexamine the question of expert influence (Breton and Proulx 2012).

This analysis, both analytical and empirical, is based on my experience as a health program editor at *La Cinquième chaîne* from 1994 to 1998[1], and will focus on a series from this period: *L'Amour en questions*. The corpus was compiled by searching through INA's audiovisual databases, and is comprised of 40 13-minute programs. The methodology combines Foucauldian discourse analysis (Foucault 1971) and dispositive analysis (Lochard and Soulages 2003), in order to focus on the logics of production,

Chapter written by Sylvie PIERRE.

1 As such, I worked on the following programs: *Attention santé Qui vive*; *Le Magazine de la santé* (producer: Igor Barrère; presenter: Michel Cymes); and numerous other documentaries on health and education. I worked as a social worker, then as a teacher of health and social sciences, before joining *La Cinquième chaîne* as a program editor.

and more specifically on the relationship between television and "experts": What type of analysis makes it possible to assert that the media considers a professional to be an expert? What criteria do the media use for choosing an expert? What logics are at work in the media's discourses?

We address the question of the "opinion leader", highlighting the ways in which the relationship between a media outlet and an expert is configured – in this case, Professor Étienne-Émile Baulieu acted as the series' "scientific guarantor". By observing how discourses are produced, and by trying to identify how they are trying to influence the audience, we will show how the Columbia School's approach (Lukasik 2021) is still relevant. We will attempt to describe the process by which the relationship between the expert and the media is constructed, thus reformulating in part Lazarsfeld's figure of the "opinion leader" (Ségur 2016). My intention is to reveal the complexity of a model that cannot be reduced to its simplified contemporary versions – this complexity being precisely what allows this model to be more than ever at the heart of media operations. In fact, there are few empirical studies that reveal how the dynamics of the relationships between professionals and opinion leaders on public television are configured.

The complexity of the issues addressed in *L'Amour en questions* – including sexuality, self-image, contraception, and abortion, etc. – should not blind us to the inherently political nature of the expert's role. As Didier Tabuteau points out:

> Health is a dual notion. It is both intimate and personal, as well as fundamentally social and collective. Health policy must be part of a dialectic between the individual and collective meanings of the notion (Tabuteau 2016, pp. 273–278).

For this reason, we are going to delve into the ethical issues that the expert's role raises. In order to grasp the complexity of this problem, this chapter will take a two-pronged approach. As a first step, we will explore the issues raised by the relationship between experts and the media by identifying the standard criteria used by the media to select an "incontestable" expert figure. The second level of analysis involves identifying the links between the expert's intrinsic qualities, the way they are portrayed and the discourse they use, as well as the logics underlying the production of a series of programs such as *L'Amour en questions*. This is a central question, because it involves analyzing the values underlying the expert's discourse.

Before examining the inner workings and particularities of the profession, it is worth taking a detour to look at the etymology of "expert". The Latin root, *expertus*, means "tried and tested". "Expert" therefore refers to a "skill acquired in a profession", to use the words of *Littré*. But the ambiguity of the function, between science and power, is revealed by *Littré*'s definition: experts are individuals who, "having acquired knowledge of certain things, are appointed to verify and decide on them".

As such, what role can the expert play in the TV series *L'Amour en questions*? What are the links between the expert and the private producer – to whom the channel delegates the production of the show – and, more generally, with television? These questions can be examined from three perspectives: first, that of the foundations which highlight the expert "authority figure", then that of the torments which reveals the "controversial" expert and finally that of the commitments which highlights the figure of the expert "committed" to a humanist approach.

3.2. The expert as both an "authority figure" and an "influencer"

A series of programs on sexuality presents the characteristics of a field calling for expertise for several reasons. On the one hand, scientific and technical knowledge is abundant and complex, and subject to ideological controversies, cultural traditions and/or social factors that oppose it (Baulieu 1994, p. 449). Advances in medicine and biology have led to radical change in individuals' relationships with their body and their development, which not only raises questions about human rights, but also requires "a better understanding of scientific progress and its potential" (Baulieu 1985, p. 4). On the other hand, the expert enjoys a kind of "legitimate power" (Weber 1922) based on their status, experience and skills, which is legitimized by their affiliation with a research institution[2]. In this way, viewers regard the expert as an "authority figure", despite research showing that many factors can lead to this being called into question (Lamy 2017, pp. 43–52). The

2 In his interviews on the series, Baulieu is presented as a Professor at the Collège de France, where he held the chair of Foundations and Principles of Human Reproduction from 1993 to 1998.

choice of an expert is therefore based on a logic of scientific truth and a discourse that must be free of any ideology, within a television industry that respects the public. In *L'Amour en questions*, this requirement is represented by the figure of Baulieu, who claims to adopt a scientific posture based on truth and the clarification of knowledge in his article "*Des progrès malentendus*" (Baulieu 1985, pp. 15–20).

The need for scientific expertise in public television is reflected in the ambiguous relationship between the expert, the producer and media support, such as television, which verifies the content and broadcasts it. The expert's legitimacy depends on their knowledge, i.e. their "acquired skill" in scientific knowledge. They are seen as a mediator between fact and the media, and are therefore in a position to propose the framework for a program[3]. In a way, they are the program's mastermind, albeit under the watchful eye of the program editor: the program editor appropriates and reports on the expert's work through media supports. The expert's second role is to produce and defend frameworks for discussion. Their scientific approach is thus inevitably confronted with choices; they are a producer of standards and, in this role, participate directly in the performativity of discourse.

On December 14, 1994, the day after it went on air, *La Cinquième*, the "channel for knowledge, education and employment", broadcast the first episode (titled *La Sexualité*) of *L'Amour en questions*. Its (clearly) stated aim was to provide "simple answers to the questions that everyone (parents, educators, and especially teenagers) have about sexuality"[4]. This positioned the series as one of the few sex-education series aimed at this particular audience on public television at the time. Baulieu appeared in five episodes as a scientific advisor. As the most interviewed personality in the series, he served as a true figure of authority, a great researcher aware of the importance of science in our lifestyles, especially for women:

> The century was about the meeting of science and women (Baulieu in the episode, *Les Questions de l'amour*).

3 *L'Amour en questions* was created and produced by Simone Harari, with Étienne-Émile Baulieu acting as the series' "scientific advisor".

4 Presentation of the program in *La Cinquième's* program magazine of 01/07/1995.

His personality as a military man (a former Resistance fighter), his humanist and universalist values, his rejection of dogmatism and his approach to science as a way to emancipate women, were all reflected in the series:

> It's very impressive for me [to] see how modern science can stimulate and set in motion a whole society, which must ask itself ethical questions and discuss women's rights (Baulieu and Fourest 2013, p. 181).

The series as a whole adopts an open-minded stance, and follows through on its objective of combating contemporary conservativism, and taboos and prejudices in particular. The show fulfilled an informative function in response to an assumed need for clear and accessible discourse on sexuality. However, the scientific backing of such an expert raises questions about the rationale behind the production of the program.

In France, the very mention of the term lobbying generally arouses suspicion. Its practice is said to be detrimental to democracy (Escurat 2016, p. 9), yet, lobbying is commonplace in the media and widely accepted. Far from being a mere fringe or taboo practice, lobbying can be beneficial to program production, provided it is in line with the missions and ethics of the TV show in question. Given its cultural heritage, the French approach has long been resistant to the participation of interest groups in the program-making process on public television (Pierre 2012).

Despite the backlash it receives in France, lobbying is neither a recent nor an exceptional phenomenon. In fact, it has existed right from the start of television, for example, television programs called "*compensées*" aired from 1951 onwards and were a form of collective advertisement that justified a general interest. Since then, it is clear that the television industry has come to terms with lobbying. At *La Cinquième chaîne*, the role of program editor was designed to limit the encroachment of lobbies on televised content. However, in reality, the television industry has done little to limit the influence of figures like Professor Baulieu, who, given his position in the political and pharmaceutical spheres, is indeed a "man of influence".

In his March 23, 1994 lecture at the Collège de France, titled "*Fondements et principes de la reproduction humaine*" (Foundations and principles of human reproduction), Baulieu clearly defined the issues at stake when it comes to information about sex:

> The duty of those who have the knowledge in this field seems to me to present it as explicitly assimilable as possible for the greatest number, without taking sides with one or other of the possible methods to be used. In this field even more than in many others, one cannot impose, but only propose. (Baulieu 1994)

The television industry recognizes the positive role that an influential player can have in the program-making process, and considers "the participation of the scientific community" to be inherent to democratic life.

A corollary of the organization of *La Cinquième chaîne* and the delegation of creation to outside producers, this change has resulted in a clear retreat from its journalistic function. An erosion which, by breaking down the boundaries between the media and private producers, tends to favor the interference of influential players in the production process. As a result, it is now accepted that experts play a part in television's public service objectives and in generating public interest. Put another way, *La Cinquième chaîne* is a television channel that no longer holds the monopoly of public service content. The dispersal of its authority, a result of "multi-level governance", reduces its room for maneuver and, in turn, multiplies the points of access to content for interest groups, thus moving from a logic of vertical governance to contractual television based on shared values. Symbolically, it is the sacrosanct French fiction of public television untouched by the figure of "influencer". All that remains is to regulate the practice, to guard against its potential abuses.

Creating educational programs about sexuality on television is in line with the mission of knowledge-based, informative television. The channel makes its approach clear:

> With a wealth of diagrams, [the show] explains the process of conception and development of a human being. The tone is didactic[5].

5 Luton, P. (1995). *La Cinquième magazine*, April 29th (p. 19).

The same article situates the project in the context of the AIDS era:

> Today, spaces for debate are opening up in the media, taboos are being broken [...] While [we know that] sex can become lethal, sexuality has been freed from its prejudices.

The program's intention was to go beyond what was being taught, including in the home environment; this affirmation has been underlined in a dedicated slogan:

> If your kids know things about sex that you didn't know they knew, don't panic, it's *La Cinquième*![6]

We find a similar tone in what we say, then, as the editor responsible for the Health Prevention programs at *La Cinquième*. This desire to "remove guilt, simplify and put ourselves in the viewers' shoes" is summed up in the title of the article in which we are interviewed: "Informing the public, a civic duty!"[7] Finally, these different stances are reflected in Jean-Marie Cavada's intentions for *La Cinquième*, which he chaired from 1994 to 1997:

> It's a unique public company where we try to apply on a daily basis the idea, so often evoked, of citizen television, [...] a real tool for popular education[8].

In the search to promote and broadcast scientific facts on public television, Jean-Marie Cavada has not forgotten the viewer:

> I think it's important that those in charge of popularizing science on television explain what it means to the public and take them on a journey of pleasure[9].

Sex education is just one area of knowledge that television has a duty to provide, if only because of the importance of scientific knowledge in society:

---

6 The insert was distributed to 22,000 partner pharmacies on AIDS Day, November 17, 1995.

7 Cuq, L. (1995). *La Cinquième magazine*, April 29th (p. 31).

8 (1995). Editorial, *La Cinquième magazine*, July 1st.

9 Speech by Jean-Marie Cavada at the 12th International Audiovisual Meeting on September 30, 1995, "*Image et Science*" round table, organized by CNRS and *La Cinième*.

> Explaining, de-dramatizing and placing science in the overall context of society is one of the fundamental roles of a TV channel dedicated to spreading knowledge and awareness[10].

The ambition of the series, and beyond that of the initial *La Cinquième* project, is therefore to define knowledge as an intangible common good, which the State, through its public channels, has a duty to make available, thus defining a programming deontology, at the risk of surprising, disturbing and provoking debate (Ozyl 2021, p. 69).

How did this series, aimed at teenagers, avoid the risk of a single discourse by "not imposing, but only proposing", as Baulieu puts it? On the one hand, the episodes are part of a clearly stated scientific discourse. The series consists of 40 episodes, which distinguish between male and female topics: menopause/andropause, female/masculine pleasure, female/masculine contraception, etc. The project's aim and approach is therefore to be exhaustive, which is confirmed by an article in the channel's program magazine:

> The ambition of the series is vast, as it also aims to serve as a catalog of reference documents […] that educational institutions or associations can use[11].

Several episodes reflect a medical approach to sexuality – with episodes such as *De la fécondation à l'embryon* (from fertilization to the embryo), and *La Stérilité* (infertility) – while others take a more individual-focused, societal approach – for example, *La Découverte du baiser* (discovering kissing), *La Paternité* (paternity) and *Le Plaisir au féminin* (female pleasure). Some episodes, such as *Garçons et filles* (boys and girls), *Vouloir un enfant* (wanting a child) and *Le Sida* (AIDS), fall somewhere between these two approaches. With the analysis of expert contributions, the psychological and even psychoanalytical approach is also addressed, without reducing sexuality to the medical sphere. The model, however, is that of "the family, based on the ties that bind a man, a woman and their children" (Baulieu 1985, p. 4), excluding gender issues at the time.

---

10 Interview with Jean-Marie Cavada in *Le Figaro*, September 1, 1995.

11 Flocon, C. (1997). Éducation sexuelle, l'amour à l'écran. *Magazine de la Cinquième*, June 28. 26, 23.

3.3. The "controversial" expert

By 1995, Baulieu had been considered a highly "controversial" figure since the 1970s by conservative circles and his peers for his links to the pharmaceutical industry as a consultant, as well as for creating the famous abortion pill, RU-486[12] or mifepristone. A specialist in steroid hormones, he is thus world-renowned for his development of antiprogesterone RU-486. In 1965, he became a scientific advisor to the president of the pharmaceutical company Roussel-Uclaf, for whom he tested the physiological effects of his synthetic molecules, including RU-486. His team then turned to research in molecular endocrinology.

In the late 1970s, he published the results of RU-486 with Roussel-Uclaf and fought for many years to obtain marketing authorization. In 1988, Roussel-Uclaf withdrew the marketing authorization it had just obtained for RU-486 due to religious and political opposition. Roussel-Uclaf finally decided to take on and exploit the product after the then Minister for Health, Claude Évin, intervened and stated that "RU-486 is the moral property of women" (Mathieu 2022, p. 348), and proposed that it be entrusted to another company. The abortion pill was authorized in France in 1988, then gradually in other countries[13]. Violent arguments ensued, with attacks coming from anti-abortionists, including within Roussel-Uclaf itself – the former president, who was very close to Pope John Paul II, accused Baulieu of being "anti-family", and "an embryo murderer". Baulieu came under attack in the USA following the launch of the RU-486 pill, where he survived an attempted bomb attack in New Orleans in 1986–1987. Conversely, he was praised by some feminist activists for RU-486, who saw it as a revolutionary, emancipatory technology that guaranteed women autonomy from doctors and their instruments (Clarke and Montini 1993, pp. 42–78).

The likelihood of monetary exchange is obviously essential with the use of an expert like Baulieu, even if the scientist is not marketing an invention. It may be tempting, in order to sell a product, to seek to influence women by extolling its merits. But other situations, such as economic ties, research

12 Molecule name for the antiprogesterone hormone responsible for the disintegration of the uterine lining, and therefore abortion.

13 From January 1, 2023, the morning-after pill was made free for all women in France, regardless of age.

contracts or consultancy sessions, can implicitly alter an expert's objectivity when confronted with a subject with which they are otherwise connected.

Numerous studies show a link of interest that influences the expert to express favor towards a product or company. The expert must therefore maintain an ethical stance, i.e. to state the truth without attempting to influence or manipulate the viewer. As we have seen, the dividing line is sometimes very fine, which is why the French Parliament passed the laws of July 1, 1998, and March 4, 2002, to provide additional deontological safeguards in order to prevent conflicts of interest among all healthcare professionals. By making actual or potential conflicts of interest public, we are certainly creating greater transparency for viewers. With *L'Amour en questions*, public television took a risk in endorsing a controversial expert on the grounds that Baulieu could offer the guarantees of a rigorous, committed and humanistic scientific stance.

However, *L'Amour en questions* did provoke an ideological controversy: the year the series was broadcast, a Catholic association orchestrated a mail campaign against the program, forcing philosopher Michel Serres, chairman of *La Cinquième*'s Scientific Advisory Board, to respond, invoking freedom of expression and the guarantee of a scientific discourse. This campaign showed that such a program, since it disturbed religious morality, had a rightful place on a public channel, as Professor Baulieu expressed very well with regard to other attacks: "Somewhere, it's recognition!" (Baulieu and Fourest 2013, p. 94 *ff.*). Here, the expert and the media came together in agreement: they had a moral duty to inform the audience, to refuse censorship, to emancipate the viewer's mind, and to foster critical thinking. Although the postal protest did not stop the series from being broadcast, neither *La Cinquième* nor any other channels ever developed a similar show aimed at providing sex education to teenagers again. As such, teenagers were left to obtain sex education from social media, where they could be exposed to pornography, cyber-violence and fake news.

3.4. The "engaged" expert

The show *Histoire de la contraception* retraces the key moments in the feminist fight for contraception. This is the societal and moral approach of the series, where the aim is to go beyond a normative, guilt-inducing discourse. In some shows, advertising is used to denounce precisely this discourse. Take *Les Règles*, for example, which aptly distances itself from advertisements for feminine hygiene products:

> Desacralized, demystified, trivialized, [menstruation] has been integrated into modern life, and the increasing number of advertisements for feminine hygiene products are just the most conspicuous manifestation of this. In this way, menstruation has become associated with images of vitality, simplicity and well-being, no doubt exaggerated, but ultimately closer to biological reality than the oppressive taboos of yesteryear. (Excerpt from *Les Règles* voice-over)

The emancipatory discourse is based on secularism and women's freedom of consciousness, and relayed by the experts interviewed:

> Personally, I often advise women to breastfeed; that said, I fully respect their wishes. If a woman doesn't want to breastfeed, it's not absolutely necessary, so she can do what she wants. (Anne de Kervasdoué, gynecologist, on the program *Le Sein*)

The decision to make Baulieu the show's expert was intended to bring a human dimension, open-mindedness, and mistrust of certain prevailing discourses, i.e. "forces of contemporary machismo in service of supporting conservative objectives" (Baulieu 1985), to *L'Amour en questions*. In *Histoire de la contraception*, gynecologist Joëlle Brunerie speaks unreservedly and denounces the medical profession's means of resisting methods of contraception:

> In France, contraception wasn't really made available and we weren't really able to run information campaigns and teach young doctors until after the Neuwirth law in 1967 [...] but minds hadn't necessarily changed [and] doctors were very conservative.

As Baulieu points out, sexuality has a humanist dimension:

> The pill has changed the status of women, perhaps more than anything since Adam and Eve. It may seem obvious to younger generations, but it was a revolution. A humanist and feminist revolution. Since feminism is a form of humanism... Humanity

> has a greater chance of happiness if couples can control their fertility and choose when to give birth. (Baulieu and Fourest 2013)

Given their presence in the public sphere, the expert thus becomes an "engaged scientist", to paraphrase Raymond Aron, and establishes themselves as a driver of action in the field of sexual health and for women's emancipation. Baulieu states on the show:

> Before the pill, women carried the burden of unwanted pregnancy alone. Allowing them to have a child when they want, and if they want, transfers power to them... The established order, that of tradition, religion and institutions, has been overturned. Separating sexuality as a first side with love, and on the other side with gender has transformed social, religious, and institutional traditions, as well as Western norms.

The mediatized expert thus appeared as a new form of "committed scientist" in the second half of the 20th century. They carried a particular message that they sought to share with the public. Étienne-Émile Baulieu remains one of the best examples of a scientist at the service of society, who used the media to educate the public on sex and sexuality. His work in the media aimed to overcome resistance from the professional sectors concerned, mobilize political and social players, and encourage viewers to adopt free and enlightened behaviors free from taboos.

Expertise in human sexuality is therefore, by function, called upon to rub shoulders with power. Sexuality has always had a political dimension, as shown by Michel Foucault (Foucault 1994): far from remaining confined to the private sphere, sexual issues are increasingly subject to the same political demands as all other social issues. But sex also produces a system of power in itself. It defines circles of professional relations, and establishes a more or less explicit hierarchy of experts.

Baulieu decided on the "chosen ones" featured on his programs, i.e. the experts who were allowed to speak on a particular subject. The power of the expert is proportionate to the appreciation that television has of its position. The influence of expertise is clearly not the same for programs on sexuality as for those on reducing long term or socially tolerated risks, such as obesity, smoking, alcoholism or road safety, and during health crises such as mad cow disease, contaminated blood or, more recently, Covid-19.

Where this is much controversy and uncertainty surrounding an issue in a democracy, decisions that affect individuals' health and (often) freedom can only be made based on scientific legitimacy. Baulieu's reference to "acceptability" clearly reflects this requirement to make scientific advances accessible to as many people as possible, by adopting an ethics of responsibility.

3.5. Conclusion

With *L'Amour en questions,* the use of scientific experts is in line with the *La Cinquième chaîne*'s ethos: to make scientific knowledge accessible to viewers. While the expert seeks to convince viewers of the merits of progress in the medical and biological sciences, they adopt an ethical and humanistic stance (Pierre 2021, pp. 33–49): a discourse of truth and respect for the public's freedom of conscience, without refraining from denouncing taboos, prejudices and conservatism.

However, the expert raises a number of issues, the least of which concerns the media's difficult task of assessing the legitimacy and trust that can be placed on an "opinion leader" in the field. The logics at work make it possible to grasp the complexity in the modes of production of discourses and images revolving around a sort of "tacit contract of trust" between the expert and the media.

3.6. References

Baulieu, E. (1985). Des progrès mal entendus. *Le Débat*, 36, 15–20.

Baulieu, E. (1994). Leçon inaugurale, chaire de fondements et principes de la reproduction humaine. Lecture, Collège de France, Paris.

Baulieu, E. and Fourest, C. (2013). *Libre chercheur*. Flammarion, Paris.

Baulieu, E., Héritier, F., Leridon, H. (1999). *Contraception : contrainte ou liberté ?* Odile Jacob, Paris.

Breton, P. and Proulx, S. (2012). Les techniques du convaincre : de l'argumentation à la manipulation. In *L'explosion de la communication : introduction aux théories et aux pratiques de la communication*, Breton, P. (ed.). La Découverte, Paris.

Charaudeau, P. (2005). *Les médias et l'information. L'impossible transparence du discours*. De Boeck, Brussels.

Clarke, A. and Montini, T. (1993). The many faces of RU486: Tales of situated knowledges and technological contestations. *Science, Technology and Human Values*, 18(1), 42–78.

Escurat, A. (2016). *Le lobbying : outil démocratique.* Fondation pour l'innovation politique, Paris.

Fassin, É. (2006). La démocratie sexuelle et le conflit des civilisations. *Multitudes*, 26, 123–131.

Foucault, M. (1971). *L'ordre du discours : leçon inaugurale au Collège de France prononcée le 2 décembre 1970*. Gallimard, Paris.

Foucault, M. (1994). *Histoire de la sexualité I. La volonté de savoir.* Gallimard, Paris.

Lamy, A. (2017). Mise en cause de l'autorité médicale et légitimation du discours d'expérience sur les forums de discussion en ligne. *Quaderni*, 93, 43–52.

Lochard, G. and Soulages, J. (2003). La parole politique à la télévision : du logos à l'ethos. *Réseaux*, 118, 65–94.

Lukasik, S. (2021). *L'influence des leaders d'opinion*. L'Harmattan, Paris.

Mathieu, M. (2022). L'avortement en France : du droit formel aux limites concrètes à l'autonomie des femmes. *Droit et société*, 111, 335–355.

Ozyl, D. (2021). L'éducation sexuelle à la télévision française. L'exemple de "L'amour en questions". *Télévision*, 12, 69–83.

Pierre, S. (2012). *Jean d'Arcy, penseur et stratège de la télévision.* INA/Médias histoire, Paris.

Pierre, S. (2021). D'une déontologie paternaliste à une éthique humaniste : Jean d'Arcy (1959–1980). *Télévision*, 12.

Schnegg, C. (2007). L'avortement médicamenteux : de la technique à l'expérience. La méthode abortive en question. *Nouvelles questions féministes*, 26(2), 60–72.

Ségur, C. (2016). Lazarsfeld (Paul). *Publictionnaire* [Online]. Available at: https://publictionnaire.huma-num.fr/notice/lazarsfeld-paul/.

Tabuteau, D. (2016). Politique de santé. In *Traité de santé publique*, Bourdillon, F. (ed.). Lavoisier, Cachan.

Weber, M. (1995). *Economie et société*. Plon, Paris [Original published 1922].

4

The Case of the Belgian Medical Reform Group and the Media (1964–1990)

4.1. Introduction

On December 23, 2021, Marius Gilbert, geographer, epidemiologist and a key figure in Belgium's management of the Covid-19 pandemic, was a guest on public service radio station *La Première*[1].

The debate concerned the government's latest measures, which much of the public deemed arbitrary. Indeed, the closure of cinemas, theaters and concert halls at a time when the situation did not justify it caused a stir among all sections of the population, including the experts of GEMS[2]. Marius Gilbert, a member of GEMS, provoked a media frenzy following his emotional disavowal of the political world:

> *Mr. Gilbert*: At the moment, there is a complete breakdown of trust. And it's now when we need it most. We need it, because Omicron is at the door, and the… I'm upset, because I'm…
>
> *François Heureux (journalist)*: Yes, you look quite upset, Mr. Gilbert…

Chapter written by Alexandra MICCICHE.

1 *La Première* is the public radio station of RTBF, the French-language radio and television broadcaster.

2 In Belgium, the GEMS group (or Covid-19 Management Strategy Expert Group), brought together medical scientists, researchers and representatives from the healthcare sector. It was responsible for making recommendations to the government on managing the pandemic.

> *M.G.*: Yes, because…
>
> *F.H.*: You're usually more measured…
>
> *M.G.*: Yes, I think that... I don't think that they [the government] realize… [And] That's the problem. They don't realize that the political bargaining that goes on at CodeCO[3] – perhaps we need to rethink this, but… – is eroding trust and, ultimately, impacts social cohesion. Because we shouldn't be surprised – excuse me – if in a week's time, alongside the extreme right, we find cultural players, we find healthcare staff, we find people across the entire population who are feeling mistreated by the way the pandemic is being managed.

"Marius Gilbert, tears in his eyes and broken voice", was the headline on the RTBF website[4] the following day. It was an emotion that the general press was also keen to emphasize. This media outing by the epidemiologist who, unlike other experts in Belgium, enjoyed a high level of sympathy (no doubt due to the usually measured nature of his statements), was relayed with vigor[5]. Far from being a flash in the pan, Gilbert's statements gave visibility to the solidarity movement which, a few days later, led to the government backtracking on these drastic measures[6].

3 The *Comité de concertation* (CodeCO) is "a body that brings together federal, regional and community ministers in an attempt to prevent or resolve conflicts of interest and certain conflicts of competence between components of the Belgian federal state". In the context of the Covid crisis, this was the political body that came to the fore in Belgium, insofar as jurisdictional conflicts were likely to impede the state's smooth management of the pandemic. See: https://www.vocabulairepolitique.be/comite-de-concertation.

4 Mathot, M., Heureux, Fr. (2021). Marius Gilbert, larmes aux yeux et voix cassée : "La rupture est totale" [Online]. Available at: https://www.rtbf. be/article/marius-gilbert-larmes-aux-yeux-et-voix-cassee-la-rupture-est-totale-10903540 [Accessed September 30, 2022].

5 See: https://www.lalibre.be/belgium/societe/2021/12/23/marius-gilbert-tres-emu-les-marchandages-politiques-aboutissent-a-des-absurdites-W5AQFJLE5JD4JJWNLAKRC4XAYE/, https://www.lecho.be/economie-politique/belgique/general/tres-emu-marius-gilbert-deplore-une-rupture-de-confiance-totale-ave-le-politique/10355558.html, https://www.lesoir.be/414127/article/2021-12-23/marius-gilbert-les-larmes-aux-yeux-la-rupture-de-confiance-avec-le-politique-est.

6 Interview with François Heureux, May 6, 2021.

While anecdotal, this episode reflects a moment of transformation of the expert's role in society, and – in Belgium at least – the emergence of the expert as a celebrity. As this very book demonstrates, we are at a major turning point in how the media treats experts' words (Rase 2020, pp. 16–17).

However, this process was set in motion long before March 2020. Indeed, experts expressing their discontent with and opposition to political decision-making processes in the media is nothing new, as evidenced by health controversies such as Chernobyl, the contaminated blood scandal or the mad cow disease outbreak. Social science researchers have been addressing these issues for several decades, with particular intensity from the 1990s onwards, when these major controversies were raging (Gilbert et al. 2015, pp. 13–17; Ollivier-Yaniv 2015, pp. 69–80). They demonstrate the extent to which the rise of media power within society has fostered the emergence of an "expertise of public debate", as well as transformed expertise itself (Campion 2017, pp. 30–32), gradually taking it "out of the scientific domain and into that of commentary" (Baygaert 2017, p. 50).

While the media have painted the Gilbert interview as an exceptional event, a historical approach to the situation reveals a more complex picture. Indeed, from a diachronic perspective, we can see how the Gilbert interview is part of a logical evolution. It is the result of, on the one hand, the increasing publicization of medicine and public health issues since the 1950s and 1960s and, on the other hand, of the liberalization of the media field (in particular public service). It also reveals the trend towards the spectacularization of information in audiovisual media in particular (Roekens 2004, pp. 108–109; Lits 2005; Marchetti 2010)

It is these changes that this chapter aims to explore, through the case of the media coverage of the *Groupe d'étude pour une réforme de la médecine* (GERM). GERM was a study group of engaged experts like Gilbert, some of whom shared a bond of filiation with him in a literal sense – his mother, health sociologist Perrine Humblet, was a member – and some in a figurative sense, as we shall see.

Although little known today, GERM left its mark on Belgian public health between the 1960s and 1990s. It was initially set up in 1964 as an informal think-tank, but following the May 68 protests and into the 1970s, it became the standard-bearer of medical dissidence in Belgium, transcending the worlds of academia, medicine and the general public. Thanks to its particular stance, GERM quickly provoked as much enthusiasm as criticism from the Belgian media. By conducting a diachronic study of GERM's media interventions, it is possible to precisely determine the balance of power between the different factions of the medical profession (of which the media can be the theater), the communication strategies that can be adopted by a group of expert protesters and the positioning of the media in relation to such an actor.

This chapter will address the following questions.

– What place does communication occupy in GERM's activity?

– Does GERM, which is in favor of a certain democratization of health, manage to adapt its messages to the general public?

– To what extent did the media actually contribute both to GERM's influence and its later disintegration in the early 1990s?

As such, this chapter will begin with an analysis of media sources – in particular those of Belgian television (primarily accused by the medical establishment of being in the pay of GERM) – followed by an examination of Thierry Poucet's surprising journey to becoming a communications officer for GERM.

4.2. GERM (1964–1990)

GERM was founded in response to the first medical strike in Belgium in April 1964, which was organized by the *Chambres syndicales de médecins* union and who defended a liberal vision of the profession. The strike was a protest against a reform on medical tariffs and, after three weeks, succeeded in sustainably imposing the principle of independence in the profession. However, not all medical professionals shared this view: for example, GERM was founded by university doctors[7] who were advocating for greater

7 These included university hospital doctors like Maurice Goldstein (1922–1996), a professor of vascular surgery at the Hôpital Saint-Pierre in Brussels; Henri Cleempoel (1924–1994), a cardiology researcher at the Université Libre de Bruxelles; and Lise Thiry (1921-), a professor of virology at the Université Libre de Bruxelles and a socialist activist.

accessibility to healthcare. From the outset, the group chose to adopt an action research approach in order to disseminate its broader vision of health policy to Belgian society: GERM rejected any hierarchical relationships in medical practice and aimed to build a medicine of solidarity against hospitalocentrism, a health democracy centered on knowledge coconstructed and shared with citizens. To achieve this, GERM advocated for abolishing the divides between medicine, interdisciplinarity and pluralism. This is why, from the outset, it has made a point of including actors from a wide range of backgrounds in its ranks, such as paramedical professions, social science researchers, sociopolitical actors and activists, etc[8].

Through this positioning, GERM's actions are highly revealing of the diversification and redistribution of knowledge in society in the second half of the 20th century, at the root of the emergence of so-called "lay" expertise, as well as the institutionalization of (activist) counter-expertise (Lascoumes 2011, pp. 221–233; Salman and Topcu 2015, pp. 164–172; Poucet and Van Dormael 2017, pp. 28–37). In Belgium, these changes took place in the first half of the 1970s, which was marked by a series of breakthroughs and fruitful reforms in the medical sphere, which GERM either spearheaded or supported. Take, for example, the movement to decriminalize abortion, embodied by the gynecologist Willy Peers, one of the group's driving forces since the 1960s; reflections on the status of the mentally ill; or the movement challenging the Medical Council in Belgium.

While active on many fronts and in a variety of areas, the group nevertheless progressively centered its action around two axes that, in its view, would completely overhaul the healthcare system by giving primary care the place it deserves. Firstly, GERM supported trial integrated health centers, and was involved in the *maisons médicales* movement – the Belgian counterpart to the French *maisons de soins* (care homes) movement. Secondly, GERM focused on health education, which often led to the group doing consultancy work at the request of those working in the field. Its work in health education resulted in GERM being recognized by the government as an official organization for continuing education from 1977 onwards. As such, the group received subsidies that enabled it to expand the scope of its activities. However, in 1987, GERM was hit by budget cuts imposed by the

8 In 1971, GERM defined the main lines of its work by publishing its "manifesto": GERM (1971). *Pour une politique de la santé*. Éditions Vie Ouvrière – La Revue Nouvelle, Brussels.

liberal government who, in the midst of an economic crisis, had little sympathy for the group's principles. In the years that followed, GERM increasingly relied on volunteer support and ultimately dissolved after its merger with the *Fédération des maisons médicales* at the dawn of the 1990s (Poucet 1989, p. 28; Poucet and Van Dormael 2017, pp. 30–35)[9].

While the *Fédération des maisons médicales* still carries this legacy, GERM's influence is largely unknown today (Hendrik and Moreau 2022, p. 52). However, former members Van Dormael and Poucet do not see this as indicating the group's failure: "GERM saw its work to be accomplished when its ideas became so ingrained that we would forget that it had been the first to formulate them" (Poucet and Van Dormael 2017, p. 37). To some extent, GERM achieved this goal. While it has often been labeled as utopian by its opponents, GERM's use of avant-garde strategies is far from merely fanciful, but has instead resulted in a series of advancements and changes. This can still be seen in the group's publications, which continue to resonate today with a certain acuity.

4.3. A group of experts… who communicate

To implement its socio-political vision, GERM not only focused its activities on specific areas, but also made a point of developing efficient communication. Indeed, the group quickly realized that it needed to disseminate its ideas to both specialized and lay audiences, so from 1966 onwards, it set about doing just that. Its communications were structured around three extremes. Firstly, it organized workshops and symposia on specific themes, including hospital organization, abortion, drug addiction, mental illness, etc. Secondly, GERM produced two types of publications that were fundamental to its communication strategy: the *Lettres d'information du GERM*, which were in-depth studies on a variety of subjects – the first issues, for example, were devoted to group medicine (issue 1), university hospitals (issue 2), and the doctor–patient relationship within teamwork (issue 6) – and, from 1978 onwards, *Actualité santé*[10], a more general-interest publication that provided factual information about GERM's activities and through which the group made its commitments loud and clear. GERM was

9 Interview with Monique Van Dormael, May 9, 2021.

10 *Actualité santé* became *Place de la santé* in 1986.

active in the media from the outset, demonstrating its determination to make its voice heard beyond academic circles[11].

4.3.1. *Thierry Poucet's "unconventional" journalistic path to journalism*

GERM was able to achieve this goal thanks in part to one of its members in particular: Poucet, who was in charge of communications from the late 1970s onwards. His resolutely committed career sheds light on the context in which the institutionalization of the "(public) health" specialty took place in the world of Belgian journalism. It also shows that, as in France, these developments in Belgium coincided with the emergence of critical and politically engaged journalism in the 1970s. The publicization of medicine was accompanied by an opening up of the medical journalistic field (dominated, in the first instance, by doctors) to outside players who specialized and trained as self-taught professionals (Marchetti 2010, p. 17).

This is the case of Poucet, who never set out to become a journalist specializing in health coverage. As he himself has said, his career path was rather "convoluted". Trained as a novelist, he began his career in 1974 as a journalist in charge of "social" issues (i.e. education, the environment, health, etc.) for French daily newspaper *La Presse*. This left-leaning general-interest paper aimed to establish itself as the Belgian equivalent of *Le Monde*, based on a cooperative model. But this was all in vain; the paper collapsed after a few years. Nevertheless, for the young journalist, his first role as head of "social issues" was "a quasi-lottery that would have a definitive impact on [his] professional destiny" (Poucet 2001, p. 108). It was in this context that he came into contact with GERM, which he later joined, being attracted by the "health democracy" model promoted by the association. So in 1977, being a conscientious objector, he had to swap his military service for civilian service in the voluntary sector, Poucet naturally chose to work with GERM, where he became its publications manager. For around 10 years, he became progressively specialized in medical and public health issues, which mirrored the gradual shift in the 1970s and 1980s from information confined to specialized columns (usually run by doctors) to

11 Activity report – Réunion statutaire du GERM du 25 février 1968, Carcob, Fonds Lemaître Fonteyne, Dossier "Peers-GERM".

increasingly politicized mainstream journalism (Marchetti 2010, pp. 55–79). This was the issue:

> which [according to him], was so vast and so interwoven with economic, cultural, social, political and ethical realities that it constituted less a specialty stricto sensu than a privileged prism for analyzing and questioning the entire functioning of modern society, particularly its claims of justice and the effective promotion of well-being. (Poucet 2001, p. 108)

4.3.2. *A group of "legitimate" experts?*

Poucet's enthusiastic commitment would eventually leave its mark on GERM's communications, as did his keen awareness of the crucial issue of media visibility. This can be seen in Poucet's various writings, which reflect his interest in public service. At that time, public service television and public service radio were indeed the stage for the power plays that pitted GERM against the medical establishment, embodied by the *Chambres syndicales* union led by Dr. André Wynen[12], a figurehead of liberal medicine.

On numerous occasions, GERM and the *Chambres syndicales* would criticize the other media appearances in their respective publications, as illustrated by this excerpt from *Actualité santé* from January 1981:

> It's important to realize that what's at stake in the incessant attacks on "non-representative groups" [issued by the *Chambres syndicales*], which RTBF has to pay the price for whenever it grants them even the slightest airtime, is a whole conception of social life in which minority speech is judged a priori to be suspect, affabulatory, and negligible. This view prevails even in journalistic circles, as illustrated by this extract from *Pourquoi Pas?* of January 8, 1981:

12 André Wynen (1923–2007) was a surgeon who graduated from the Université libre de Bruxelles. In 1963, he joined the *Chambres syndicales*, which had been founded a year earlier by doctors from near Liège and Luxembourg. He quickly became the figurehead of the group, and remained so until the early 1990s (Schrijvers 2005, p. 72).

> [...] Today, 300 doctors are making it known that they refuse to pay their dues to the Order [of physicians], and we can deduce that this is a reflection of the medical profession as a whole, at least if we are to believe the repercussions given to this information by the RTBF and a section of the daily press concerned above all not to be suspected of lukewarm protest. (Poucet 1981, p. 4)[13]

These quarrels raised the question of the legitimacy of dissenting expert speech in the media and public arena, as well as the effects of the media field on the functioning of the social world of medicine and public health that also emerged.

4.4. GERM on the small screen

A dive into the television archives dealing with GERM sheds light, within the limits of the available elements, on this pervasive influence of the media field on the fields of medicine and public health, especially when their very purpose is to open up scientific knowledge. Did GERM manage to combine accessible healthcare with accessible discourse? Did it succeed in adapting its messages to a television medium that was increasingly driven by a logic of proximity? In this section, I will attempt to answer these questions through three case studies that seemingly illustrate both the communication strategies used by GERM's members, and the changes that took place in Belgian public television.

GERM's very first intervention took place in the context of what Umberto Eco conceptualized as "paleo-television", which broadcast didactic content to spectator-students confined to a certain passivity (Cassetti and Odin 1990). A thousand miles from the vibrant and emotional Gilbert or the engaged and exalted Poucet, Henri Cleempoel, a doctor at Saint-Pierre

13 In 1980–1981, hundreds of doctors, led by GERM and others, demonstrated their opposition to the Order of Physicians (Belgium), the regulatory body for the practice of the profession, by refusing to pay their subscriptions.

hospital in Brussels and a founding member of GERM, pleaded for objective and dispassionate expertise in an interview with RTB television news at an economic conference organized in Charleroi in January 1966:

> We believe that one of the most urgent things (among others) that we can do here in Belgium is to replace passion with reason, because in recent years, medical problems have aroused a great deal of passion, both in the medical world and among the general public, and we believe that this is unjustified, that there is a way to organize a healthcare system that is profitable in health, social, economic and scientific terms, based solely on objective, dispassionate scientific research, untainted by political or other passions[14].

This speech, which embodied the concept of expertise defended by GERM from the outset, contrasted with the position taken some 10 years later by Élisabeth Wollast[15], who was also a founding member of the group and taught public health at the Université libre de Bruxelles. In a TV news report on GERM's stance, she did not hesitate to take a stand against the *Chambres syndicales des médecins*, which had just started its second medical strike, and which would affect the country for almost a month between December 1979 and January 1980:

> *Voice-over*: "When you only know how to bandage...", that's what prompted GERM (*Groupe d'étude pour une réforme de la médecine*) to speak out against the strike notice issued by the *Chambres syndicales des médecins* on December 21.
>
> *[Elisabeth] Wollast*: While the *Chambres syndicales des médecins's* bogus arguments – well, I'd say most of them – are supposedly aimed at the patient's well-being, these arguments are actually concealing the personal (let's say medical) and professional interests that its doctors are aiming for[16].

There is a world of difference between these two interviews. For, even if Wollast's stance remained that of an expert analyzing and deconstructing the

14 RTB (1966). Interview with Henri Cleempoel. *9,000,000*, January 3rd, Sonuma.

15 Professor, Faculty of Public Health.

16 RTBF (1979). Interview with Élisabeth Wollast. *JT*, November 15th, Sonuma.

situation – the impersonal form (the use of the pronoun "*on*" in French) and the nuance brought to the remarks ("well, I'd say most of them") bear witness to this – it is clear that GERM, in granting this interview, is letting itself be caught up in the "political passion" that Henri Cleempoel blamed 10 years earlier. Despite the fact that these two interviews were given by two different personalities, they seem to serve as evidence of GERM's stance, to which the politicization that swept through society in general from 1968 onwards and the emergence of an impertinent, critical journalism that followed (embodied within GERM by Poucet). Behind-the-scenes documents produced by the group tend to confirm this change: during the 1970s, GERM's intervention in political debates was on the minds of its board of directors[17].

While GERM managed to keep pace with the changes in television in the 1970s, it seems that in the 1980s it was unable to meet the challenges posed by the emergence of neo-television, which brought with it a new relationship with the viewer, marked by an increased closeness and complicity. It seems that GERM's experts were not able to forge this kind of relationship with viewers; they struggled to engage the audience, and to produce more accessible content. And this was where the problem lay, as Poucet would go on to explain years later:

> They [GERM's experts] were brilliant at devising high-level alternatives to the prevailing humdrum, but at the same time they overlooked the importance of reflecting on the basic conditions under which unmotivated players would adhere to their models. If they have sinned in their often clairvoyant struggles, it was first and foremost due to a kind of sociodynamic naivety. As idealistic land democrats, they bet everything on the transformative power of thought and words, and didn't sufficiently explore the thankless strategies of mobilizing the non-activist actors who made up the bulk of the battalion, halfway between activists for distributive progress and activists for the protection, if not the extension, of privileges. (Poucet 2001, p. 124)

17 Activity Report – Réunion statutaire du GERM du juin 8, 1975, pp. 2–5, Carcob, Fonds Lemaître Fonteyne, Dossier "Peers-GERM"; Résultats de l'enquête menée auprès des lecteurs des publications du GERM, mars 1980, CARHOP, Fonds GERM, Dossier 8.

In this respect, GERM's last appearance on public television was particularly revealing of the difficulties it was facing with promoting its message to the general public in the late 1980s. In a TV interview for the 201st "textbook", Lise Thiry provoked a real outburst by revealing the behind-the-scenes details of the interview:

> *Journalist*: GERM regularly publishes a series of "textbooks" that have just passed the 200-issue mark. Issue 201 is called *Clés pour le biofutur* and is devoted to biotechnology. It's written by [you] Lise Thiry, Professor of Microbiology at the Université Libre de Bruxelles' Faculty of Medicine, and it reads in a subtitle: "This is a short guide to the technological changes underway for the use of curious laypeople". So it's a work of popularization … Is that right?
>
> *Lise Thiry*: I heard you say [earlier] that you didn't think that it was very accessible to the general public. If I wanted to be very blunt, perhaps I'd say that one of the aims is for parents who are up to the conversation to talk with their children at the table[18].

Despite this assertion, the rest of the interview, which lasts almost eight minutes and is very dense, does not entirely prove the presenter wrong: although her words are intended to be educational, they are far from being accessible to everyone.

4.5. Conclusion

What insights does this case study provide? Firstly, it allows us to outline several concomitant developments in terms of publicization and mediation of medicine and health during the second half of the 20th century. We can clearly see how the changes we have observed in the field of medical and health information in Belgium seem to mirror those observed in France by sociologist Dominique Marchetti: for example, the gradual unbundling of this type of information from the 1970s onwards under the effects of the politicization of health issues, as well as the opening up of the field of expertise to the field of journalism, and vice versa. We can also observe

18 RTBF (1987). Interview with Lise Thiry. *JT*, July 9th, Sonuma.

another important change highlighted by Marchetti in our analysis of GERM: the mediating and transformative power of the media field. While GERM was initially in step with television, which afforded it social visibility and on the basis of which it constructed its messages, it was unable to keep up with its evolution and changing relationship with the viewer, and suffered as a result. This was duly noted by Poucet, who saw the media (public service broadcasting in particular) as a place for democratic debate between citizens (Poucet 2001, pp. 113–127; Marchetti 2010, pp. 159–169).

Ultimately, what is the link between Gilbert's words and those of GERM's experts? This television representation of GERM, if we put it in perspective with the media coup of Gilbert, allows us to nuance the question of the place of the opinion of experts in the media by historicizing it, and to highlight the increasingly close relationships that unite the field of media with that of science and politics in the second half of the 20th century. More broadly, it highlights the need for official institutions within our society that can bring together politicians, scientists and citizens, in order to debate decisions on public health issues. This was already advocated by GERM in the 1970s (GERM 1971, pp. 88–92), and by historian Harry Marks in 1999 in one of his landmark works, *La Médecine des preuves* (Marks 1999, p. 343). In the current context, public service media could more prominently take on the role of an institutional intermediary. This seems to be what seems to animate certain RTBF journalists, such as Arnaud Ruyssen, who recently asserted that the next challenge facing journalists and scientists post-pandemic would be to offer programs that make the processes involved in the construction of more intelligible scientific knowledge, in order to annihilate the growing mistrust of scientists and experts that has been apparent since the spring of 2020[19]. It seems that we have come full circle, yet the debate remains unresolved.

4.6. References

Baygaert, N. (2017). Les mutations de l'expertise face à l'impératif de performance médiatique. *La Revue Nouvelle*, 3(3), 50–54.

Campion, B. (2017). Ce que les médias font à l'expertise. Quels enjeux pour l'expertise médiatique ? *La Revue Nouvelle*, 3(3), 30–35.

19 See: http://www.youtube.com/watch?v=oXssFxkJ3-g.

Cassetti, F. and Odin, R. (1990). De la paléo- à la néo-télévision. Approche sémio-pragmatique. *Communications*, 51, 9–26.

Germ (1971). *Pour une politique de la santé*. Editions Vie Ouvrière, Brussels.

Gilbert, C., Henry, E., Jouzel, J.N. (2015). L'expertise sous le regard des sciences sociales. In *Dictionnaire critique de l'expertise. Santé, travail, environnement*, Gilbert, C., Henry, E., Jouzel, J.N. (eds). Presses de Sciences Po, Paris.

Hendrik, A. and Moreau, J.L. (2022). GERM. In *De A à Z, histoire(s) du mouvement des maisons médicales*, Hendrik, A. and Moreau, J.L. (eds). Fédération des Maisons Médicales-ORAM, Brussels.

Lascoumes, P. (2011). Savoirs, expertises et mobilisations. In *Savoirs experts et profanes dans la construction des problèmes publics*, Damay, L., Denis, B., Duez, D. (eds). Facultés Universitaires Saint-Louis, Brussels.

Lits, M. (2005). Spectacularisation du politique. *Recherches en Communication*, 24.

Marchetti, D. (2010). *Quand la santé devient médiatique : les logiques de production de l'information dans la presse*. Presses universitaires de Grenoble, Grenoble.

Marks, H. (1999). *La médecine des preuves*. Synthélabo, Essonne.

Ollivier-Yaniv, C. (2015). La communication publique sanitaire à l'épreuve des controverses. *Hermès, La Revue*, 73, 69–80.

Poucet, T. (1981). Wynen et la RTB : la grogne d'un privilégié. *Actualité Santé*, 28(29), 2–5.

Poucet, T. (1989). Dissidences médicales : il était une fois en Belgique… *Agora*, 9, 23–32.

Poucet, T. (2001). Petit examen clinique des pratiques d'information. In *Santé, hôpitaux et médias*, Désir, D. (ed.). Éditions de l'Université de Bruxelles, Brussels.

Poucet, T. and Van Dormael, M. (2017). 1964–1990 : le GERM, pour un système de santé solidaire. *Politique, revue belge d'analyse et de débat*, 101, 28–37.

Rase, C. (2020). Paroles d'experts. *FNRS.News, Le magazine du fonds de la recherche scientifique*, 119, 16–17.

Roekens, A. (2004). Jalons pour une histoire de la RTBF. In *RTBF – 50 ans. L'extraordinaire jardin de la mémoire*, Hanot, M. (ed.). Musée Royal de Mariemont, Brussels.

Salman, S., Topçu, S. (2015). Expertise profane. In *Dictionnaire critique de l'expertise. Santé, travail, environnement*, Henry, E., Gilbert, C., Jouzel, J.-N., Marichalar, P. (eds.), Presses de Sciences Po, Paris.

Schrijvers, K. (2005). De artsenstaking van 1964. *Cahiers d'Histoire du Temps Présent*, 16, 57–89.

PART 2

Lay Expertise versus Scientific Expertise

5

Presenting the Expert's Ethos in the Magazine Press: "Dr. H's Column"

5.1. Introduction

The family press – understood here as magazines aimed at expectant young parents – calls on experts, obstetrician–gynecologists, child psychiatrists and pediatricians. With this in mind, we hypothesized that the statements or discourses of these experts could constitute a corpus of testimonies of their professional *ethos* and their relationships with their patients and their patients' families.

One such example of a family press publication is *Famili*, which was first published in 1993 as a monthly, although it has been a bi-monthly for some years now. The magazine offers a wealth of advice for the expectant mother, including advice on childcare and adjusting to life with a baby, as well as health files which feature interviews with specialists, and columns by doctors with whom the magazine regularly collaborates. Our interest was in the latter.

Between 2013 and 2016, *Famili* ran an original column for young parents or parents-to-be – the likes of which we have not found in any competing magazine. The column was written by Dr. Thierry Harvey, head of the

Chapter written by Laurence CORROY and Émilie ROCHE.

maternity ward at Diaconesses Hospital[1], and called "*La chronique du Dr H*" (Dr. H's column) – a play on the first letter of his name and the hospital. In his column, Dr. H reflects on his experiences and speaks on his relationships with his patients, which is why we created our corpus from all of his columns. In each edition, he presents a theme and explores it through his personal experience. He has written 16 columns for *Famili*[2] magazine.

Unlike the magazine's other discursive spaces, the discourses of the doctor and his patient, the pregnant woman, are reproduced in the magazine – a study we felt would be fruitful in terms of the representation and analysis of expert discourse. The challenge here was to understand both how medical expertise and the expert are presented, as well as the possible evolution of the gynecologist/patient relationship over the past decade, in a context in which relationships between gynecologists and patients have been called into question, notably via testimonial sites on the Internet (Schantz et al. 2021).

5.2. When medical expertise is embodied: the case of Dr. H

Numerous scientific works on pregnancy and birth make it possible to place these discourses in a historically and socially situated discursive environment; it has been shown that pregnancy and birth are socially constructed issues that largely transcend the theme of human reproduction. Two areas have changed the most significantly over the last 50 years: family structures, insofar as they give a place to the child, and medical advances linked in gynecology and obstetrics:

> Thus, when taken in its broadest sense, birth is undoubtedly one of the most intimate domains – in terms of the way it changes women's relationships to their bodies, the underlying project, adjusting to life with the newborn and parenthood – without its public and political dimension being called into question. (Charrier and Clavandier 2013, p. 12)

1 The hospital group Diaconesses Croix Saint-Simon, was formed from the merger of two hospitals in 2003, including the Diaconesses de Reuilly hospital, which had been part of the public hospital service since 1976. In 2016, the maternity ward had approximately 40 nurses on staff and delivered 2,558 babies.

2 Since 2018, 14 columns have been published on the *Famili* website, magicmaman.com, with no indication that they were published in the magazine in the past.

By moving out of the home and becoming a medical specialty, the process of procreation has migrated from the private to the public sphere. For researchers in the social sciences, the medicalization of pregnancy marks this shift from private to public and puts women's place in the world under pressure:

> Medicalization has played a crucial role in the contemporary history of birth because it brings together several dynamics leading to the transformation of birth from a private fact to a public fact, while renewing the setting of relations between men and women, particularly in its professional side. (Ibid., p. 14)

The very existence of magazines that focus on pregnancy and early childhood is part of this process at the forefront between the intimacy of the family unit (in the making or established) and its assumption of responsibility by society. These magazines reflect both customs and norms, and disseminate socio-discursive narratives by featuring doctors and patients. In *Famili*, Dr. H serves as both the mediator and the embodiment of medical expertise: he is a department head with decades of experience, and an expert figure who is capable of breaking taboos. In 2017, *Famili* ceased publication. It resumed publication the following year under the name *magicmaman*, with a website of the same name. The site features the Dr. H columns that were previously published in *Famili*, and presents Dr. H as follows:

> How not to induce childbirth, how should we set limits to assisted reproduction technology (ART), should you have your other children with you at the ultrasound… In each issue of *magicmaman*, **Dr. Thierry Harvey** shares his thoughts of the day. Better known to readers as **Dr. H,** he mixes humor with gravitas to discuss everything that affects the **lives of new and expectant mothers** in one way or another. And he's not afraid to talk about it all, taking the taboo out of pregnancy!
>
> Dr. Thierry Harvey has been an obstetrician–gynecologist for over 30 years and is **head of the Diaconesses maternity hospital** in Paris. When he's not helping young women deliver their babies, he is talking to us about moments in his life as a doctor and what it's like working in the maternity ward. His

> outspokenness allows him to tackle any subject without concession, much to our delight![3]

Emerging in the background, we can start to identify the characteristics of Dr. H's medical *ethos*: namely, audacity in his daring to tackle "taboo subjects", humor, know-how informed by his extensive experience (helping to deliver babies) and the knowledge of which he is the custodian (opting for a serious tone).

5.3. Asymmetry in doctor–patient discourse

In the texts studied, the discourse is presented as a verbal exchange, in which Dr. H presents his own perspectives as well as his patients' views. The reproduced dialogues create a real effect that draws the reader into the discourse since they immediately identify themselves with the narrative figure of the mother-to-be. In this case, the doctor as third-party mediator produces a discourse which appears (since it is reported) like a real-life interaction, and in which the main speaker (Dr. H himself, and, beyond that, as discourse analysis, *Famili* magazine) has all the power. In line with the work of Catherine Kerbrat-Orecchioni and Sophie Moirand, we have analyzed argumentation in conversational exchanges and press discourse.

While Dr. H gives the pregnant woman a voice, it is essentially only within their role as a patient. By presenting his consultations, Dr. H vindicates Marty Laforest, who explains:

> The numerous studies carried out on the interactions between health professionals and consultants have well documented how, on a strictly interactional level, "power" is constructed and the strategies used by patients – who are in a subordinate position in these interactions – to make their voices heard. The consultation is an unequal interaction: asymmetrical in terms of who has the right to speak, the choice of subjects discussed, and the specialization of types of intervention. (Laforest 2012, p. 96)

The magazine functions as an echo chamber: affirming and reaffirming social norms and representations. The ways in which woman are reduced to the figure of the patient also led us to analyze the effect on the relationships

3 Bold terms have been preserved from the original text.

these women have with their bodies. In this respect, Sarah Lécossais' work on the way in which serial fictions put pregnancy into words is illuminating. She explains that "these narratives are also gender narratives that renew and confirm the association of women with 'Nature' and the assignment of their gender – processes aimed at reaffirming a gender hierarchy that is unfavorable to women" (Lécossais 2017, p. 158). Lécossais emphasizes the extent to which the advice and recommendations that function as diktats, and even the prohibitions relayed to pregnant women, are part of a Foucauldian dynamic of discipline and coercive normalization of pregnant bodies.

In our examination of the status of the pregnant woman in Dr. H's column, we can identify four main topics (presented below in order of recurrence): childbirth and the period afterwards; pregnancy follow-up, which includes the behaviors to be observed during pregnancy and consultations; the place of the father; and lastly, reflections on assisted reproductive technology (ART).

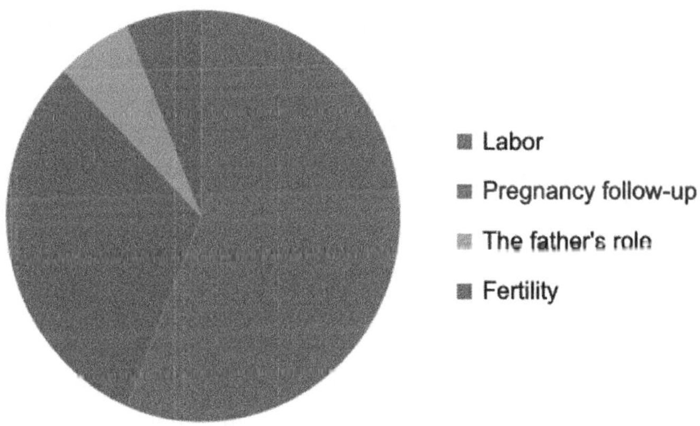

Figure 5.1. *Topics covered in Dr. H's column. For a color version of this figure, see www.iste.co.uk/corroy/health.zip*

In these columns, elements concerning the parents and the baby (born or unborn) are interwoven, as well as a dramatization of themselves and the relationships they forge with their patients. We have therefore selected all the passages in Dr. H's columns in which the doctor refers to his patients (and, by extension, his readers), as well as to his own experience. This is a personal experience, a special case of a recognized doctor with a media platform of choice.

5.4. Vulnerable pregnant women

Most of Dr. H's columns begin with reflections from his patients, who help him introduce the subject he wishes to address. This in turn helps us to understand how he perceives his patients and how he reports on what he has to say. The special relationship that develops between doctor and patient parturients is often portrayed as capricious and frivolous, subject to irrational desires, to which the doctor responds by using reason, drawing on his medical experience and scientific studies. Faced with young women under stress, but quick to forget at Christmas time the dietary restrictions, or the harmful effects of products with fake sugars, steeped in beliefs rather than scientific facts, manipulated and made to feel guilty by the discourse they hear from all sides, the gynecologist has an authoritative role, sometimes benevolent, sometimes more firm, reminding them of dietary restrictions or vaccination requirements. These injunctions are fueled by the discourses of certain psychologists or psychoanalysts, asserting:

> Every pregnant woman is more or less always in a different psychological and psychosomatic state from her usual one, due to having another being inside her, who also modifies her interlocutors in the know. We can call this state "fragile", or more open and accessible, more transparent or more opaque, more vulnerable and stronger. In other words, a pregnant woman has always been and in every culture the bearer of paradoxes. (Aubert-Godard 2002, p. 40)

> A classic consultation? Take this plea from one pregnant woman hooked on Japanese cuisine: "Doctor, this is horriiible, I'm not going to be able to eat sushi for nine months!" You can replace "sushi" with steak tartare, foie gras, cheese… (*Famili*, April–May 2015, p. 121)

> You understand, Doctor, I prefer more intimate maternity units, which is what you're advising me, the giant over medicalized type III structures, it's not for me… (*Famili*, December 2013, p. 118)

> Three days, doctor! Give me three more days to give birth naturally, then you can induce me. Sometimes, my practice takes on the air of a Moroccan souk, but where the negotiators

> are more convincing than carpet merchants from across the Mediterranean. (*Famili*, April–May 2014, p. 132)

> Are you past the 35th week in your pregnancy? Your feet are swollen, your thighs are touching and you can't sleep on your stomach anymore? You're ripe for alternative therapies: grandma's remedies intended to trigger your labor. (*Famili*, October–November 2015, p. 132)

> The full moon does NOT make you give birth! It feels so good to write that. Thirty years I've been saying this to my patients, who are panic-stricken when I'm not at the maternity ward on "werewolf days". But to no avail: pregnant women are stubborn creatures. (*Famili*, June–July 2013, p. 144)

Lécossais has also highlighted narrative patterns that infantilize the pregnant woman and dispossess her of her body:

> The pregnant woman is not a being of reason; she is a being of flesh and blood, hormones and impulses. Yet it is indeed through language that women are reminded of their gender, as words make effective the idea of a particular feminine nature. (Lécossais 2017, pp. 166–167)

Hormonal variations, body transformations and potential side effects women can experience make them fragile, thanks to their gender. She goes on to point out that while "pregnancy is no longer considered a disease, it remains a discursive moment of production of inequalities presented as natural between men and women, no longer based on 'temperament', but on hormones" (ibid.).

In Dr. H's discourse, he reaffirms a policy of governing women's bodies, and also reflects on the conflict between patient and doctor. While the obstetrician has the final say over the pregnant woman's body, according to Dr. H, we can see the tensions that result from this assumption of power play here:

> This morning, I was again called a "dirty episiotor". A woman, who had just given birth to her second child, a beautiful, healthy 3kg baby (her first child, weighing 3.5kg, had been born

> without an episiotomy), almost gouged my eyes out because I had dared to deviate from her "birth plan", which obviously did not include my surgical scalpel… (*Famili*, October–November 2014, p. 144)

> How many crying young mothers have I comforted after a C-section or epidural birth? Because they were overwhelmed with happiness? Not at all. I've consoled these extraordinary young mothers for having "stolen their birth". What a curious expression. (*Famili*, October–November 2013, p. 130)

> Because Hollywood films and real life are two different things. It's better to have a C-section go wrong than a natural birth go wrong. But accepting this medical choice also means celebrating your happy ending: you and your baby, both in good health! (*Famili*, February–March 2015, p. 121)

The expression of the women's discourse and that of the doctor are causally related: while the doctor has no decision-making power, the situation may become life-threatening. Indeed, researchers working on the sociology of birth have shown that "the intimization of the relationship to birth is reflected in an increasingly technical and medicalized healthcare landscape, even in the places where childbirth takes place" (Charrier and Clavandier 2015, pp. 27–28). These researchers underline the obvious paradox between the increasingly sophisticated medicalization of maternity facilities, while at the same time promoting for each couple an individualized birth to come, free from technical and health constraints. These tensions are at the heart of feminist research calling for a renegotiation of the place of the female body and patients' rights (Froidevaux-Metterie 2022, p. 22).

5.5. The midwife, or the temptation of the creator?

It is clear that for Dr. H, the doctor must know how to say no: to oppose the unreasonableness of (new) mothers and parents with medical reason for the sake of the well-being of the pregnant woman and her baby, "to save a life, sometimes two" (*Famili*, October–November 2013, p. 130). Is the obstetrician–gynecologist part of the temptation of the creator here? "Only the person who has his hand on your perineum when your little one arrives can make the decision whether or not to proceed with an episiotomy", he writes (*Famili*, October–November 2014, p. 144). As he describes it himself:

> It's not that I want to deprive these ladies of a "natural" birth for the sake of it. Or because I'm a sadist! But you have to know when to stop and be the bad guy who says no, solely for the good of the patients and their little one. (*Famili*, April–May 2014, p. 132)

The doctor's image of himself emerges through the texts: he is the first line of defense for the unborn child, standing in the way of obscurantism, preconceived ideas and unreasonable demands from future parents, and ready to do anything for his patients' good health. For example, he removed a vending machine that offered diet products, which are bad for his patients, at the risk of upsetting his entire department. He chooses what he feels is best for the health of the mother and child, and there is no debate about it. As he describes himself, he is the one who lays down the law as a quasi-paternal figure:

> So, sometimes I say no. No, I can't carry out this ART method. Because, as a doctor, I can't support this idea of a child at any price. I'm a father, and even a grandfather. I feel in my bones what it's like to want a child. But feeling compassion is not the same as diagnosing. And accepting to treat some people with ART would be an unethical medical decision, which I can't accept. I can't do that. It hurts, it may seem unfair to couples, but this decision is motivated by a fundamental consideration: the duty not to kill. (*Famili*, December 2015–January 2016, p. 136)

> I always allow the mother to choose her birth plan if everything is in place to ensure her safety and that of the baby. If this is not the case, I won't budge. (*Famili*, June–July 2013, p. 144)

There seems to be a double asymmetry: the scientist vis-à-vis the novice, and the dominant place of the doctor over the body. Chiara Quagliariello explains that the symbolic violence in women's submission to doctors' discourses leads to obstetrical violence (Quagliariello 2017; El Kotni and Quagliariello 2021). As noted in the field study by Hardy et al. on the follow-up of pregnancies and the choice of the caregiver, "the risk then becomes a challenge of the power relationship between caregivers and parturients" (2015, p. 67).

This position seems to be widely shared by obstetricians. Stéphanie Saint-Amant, a birth rate specialist, observes that the rate of induced births and C-sections is constantly on the rise worldwide, while there is a drop in the weekend birth rate. In 2013, according to the Peristat study, 11% of C-sections in France took place before the onset of labor, and 50% of C-sections performed in Europe were planned. This leads Peristat to question the benefits of scheduling births surgically at such a scale: "The conceptual construct that legitimizes such a lax and generalized conception, scheduling birth rests on a representation of pregnancy as a process associated with an expiration date, always liable to shooting yourself in the foot, to jeopardizing its fruit" (Saint-Amant 2015).

Dr. H's ability to say no to requests he considers unreasonable or dangerous does not prevent him from developing a special relationship with his patients. When he talks about them, there is evident tenderness: "I don't want to steal their birth. But I'm always happy that in the end it's them who steal the show!" he exclaims (*Famili*, October–November 2013, p. 130).

They are "extraordinary young moms", "strong fighters", as well as his "adored patients", his "dear pregnant women". By extension, the magazine's readers are also referred to as its "dear readers", or "cherished readers":

> I've been delivering babies for three decades. And it's just like the first day. The miracle of life, even for a tough guy like me, still blows my mind. (*Famili*, June–July 2013, p. 144)

So this "tough guy", as he likes to call himself, a father and grandfather in life, is also the one who brings babies into the world. He embodies life, and must protect it at all costs.

Within this unique, special bond, which culminates in the birth of a healthy, living child, there is little room for any other characters. The presence of other children is strongly discouraged in the consultation rooms since they can become agitated and disrupt the gynecologist's concentration, or that of the parents. And even if a child sits quietly on their father's lap, they distract the doctor from what is, in his eyes, the most important thing in the room: the pregnant woman and the child in her womb.

5.6. The father's role

In this privileged relationship between patients and their obstetrician–gynecologist, little room is given to the father. The doctor embodies an authority figure: the one who dictates the law, the one who brings babies into the world. Dr. H rarely mentions the father in his columns. His place is with his wife: praising her and telling her that she is exceptional. For the rest, the father must remain on the sidelines.

However, Dr. H devotes one column entirely to the father, titled "*De la place du père*" (August–September 2013, p. 121). The article takes issue with "the trend for this ridiculous practice of skin-to-skin contact between infants and their fathers". While Dr. H advocates maternal skin-to-skin contact, which enables the child to feel "the warmth as well as the smell and heartbeat" of its mother, he considers the same practice strange for fathers, with their hairy torsos and "unfamiliar heartbeat":

> Do today's dads need this artifice to take their place as fathers? With too much desire for parity, we're forgetting its nature. (*Famili*, August–September 2013)

Dr. H also takes issue with the father's desire to cut the umbilical cord:

> Cutting the cord, a genuine medical act, is also one of those acts taken over by some dads. (*Famili*, August–September 2013)

He urges them to just be fathers and husbands and "not act as mothers or surrogate gynecologists". He ends the article with these words.

> Then I can finally stop having nightmares about yet another "modern" father asking me to take care of his wife's episiotomy stitches… (*Famili*, August–September 2013)

In this almost exclusive relationship between the mother-to-be and her gynecologist, Dr. H sees the husband as a competitor who dreams of stealing the doctor's power in a Promethean style act – to take his place. For the father-to-be, "being there for your child", he claims, "doesn't necessarily mean being active". The only one entitled to "take control" of a patient's body (to borrow a phrase from Dr. H) is the doctor. Any intrusion by the father-to-be is at best tolerated, seen as an interference in the special, precious and exclusive relationship the doctor builds with his patients. But are there any reservations or limits to medical omnipotence?

5.7. The limits of medical power

Nature is evoked, constraining both patients and doctors. Medical ethics for Dr. H means submitting to the laws of nature and refusing demands that he considers unreasonable in view of the constraints it imposes. The laws of nature direct medical ethics in order to avoid unnecessarily endangering the lives of mother and child: such as ART for a woman who is too old, or a vaginal delivery if the unborn child is in danger or if the woman's pelvis is too narrow. The doctor must then explain to their patients the limits of their power, constrained by the laws of nature. It is the doctor's role to remind patients of the ideal age for procreation and the restrictions that must be respected to ensure a healthy pregnancy.

The second limit to his power, which Dr. H mentions, is based on material contingencies: the relationship with time, always limited, that medical teams have and that can sometimes hinder good communication with future parents. In a hospital, with all the difficulties that teams have to deal with, it is not always easy to be sure that information has been understood and assimilated. That is why Dr. H repeatedly urges his readers to talk to their gynecologist and midwife beforehand about what they want, and what they are curious about.

Although the baby is not an active player, they are nevertheless the heart of the relationship between mother and doctor. It is for the baby's sake that the doctor makes his recommendations during pregnancy and his decisions in the delivery room.

5.8. Conclusion

Informative magazines aimed at parents produce injunctive discourses that create norms, raise the question of gender inequalities and reproduce a bio-power that is stated quite clearly, but which is barely visible. We can also identify tensions that testify, if not to a kind of resistance of women, at least to their desire to start a conversation around their pregnancy and their body. Dr. H's column presents an asymmetrical relationship between the doctor – an authoritative figure of expertise, who lays down the law, vis-à-vis the pregnant woman. Should we see this as an "epistemic injustice" that discounts women's experiences and voices (Schantz et al. 2021), or as an unintentional disregard for patients' intimate experiences (Briex 2022)?

Two forms of *ethos* are at play, sometimes expressed as complementary, but more frequently caught up in a strong antagonism. The *desiderata* of patients are not disregarded, but they take a back seat. The autonomy of parturients consequently seems to be restricted. Here, inequality of knowledge seems to be coupled with gender inequality (Sen 2000). As Courtial and Le Dreff (2004, p. 118) state "[d]octors believe they have achieved perfection, zero risk, while the price to pay is the substitution of medical childbirth for physiological childbirth, absolute conformity to the medical standard". This substitution undoubtedly partly explains the reactions that the doctor reports from young, dissatisfied mothers, who express the feeling of having been dispossessed of their childbirth. We have observed paradoxical effects within the discourse of the contradiction between the "birth plans" evoked, but quickly contradicted by medical requirements, i.e. of a nature domesticated by the medical, but a nature nonetheless summoned by the doctor to dismiss the father or to disqualify a desire for a child deemed inappropriate.

While the discourse given by the obstetrician on their practices are individual, are they asymptomatic? The emergence in the public debate of obstetric violence and the rise of testimonies from women who have the impression of having been dispossessed of their bodies raise the question of a narrative and social practices at work today. Amina Yamgnane, head of maternity at the American Hospital of Paris, calls into question the professional training of gynecologists and pleads for a "relationship-based approach to childbirth" (2018).

5.9. References

Aubert-Godard, A. (2002). L'aventure de la grossesse, aujourd'hui. *Laennec*, 50, 38–63.

Briex, M. (2022). Post-partum animal triste. *Spirale*, 101(1), 39–49.

Canevet, J.P., Catimel, B., Clautour, L., Hardy, C., Jourdain, M. (2015). Grossesses à suivre, les déterminants de l'usage de l'offre territoriale de soins périnataux. *Recherches familiales*, 12, 57–70.

Charrier, P. and Clavandier, H. (2013). *Sociologie de la naissance*. Armand Colin, Paris.

Charrier, P. and Clavandier, H. (2015). La naissance en mutation, un enjeu pour la sociologie ? *Recherches familiales*, 12, 165–174.

Corroy, L. (2022). *L'éducation aux médias en Europe, histoire, enjeux et perspectives*. L'Harmattan, Paris.

Corroy, L. and Chauzal-Larguier, C. (eds) (2023). *Patients, Caregivers and Doctors: Devices, Issues and Representations*. ISTE Ltd, London, and John Wiley & Sons, New York.

Corroy, L. and Ricaud, P. (2019). *Utopies et médias de masse*. ISTE Editions, London.

Courtial, J.P. and Le Dreff, G. (2004). Analyse de récits de femmes enceintes. *Santé publique*, 16, 105–121.

El Kotni, M. and Quagliariello, C. (2021). L'injustice obstétricale. Une approche intersectionnelle des violences obstétricales. *Cahiers du Genre*, 71(2), 107–128.

Froidevaux-Metterie, C. (2022). La nouvelle bataille de l'intime. *Sciences Humaines*, 343(1), 22–25.

Hardy, C., Jourdain, M., Catimel, B., Clautour, L., Canévet, J.P. (2015). Grossesses à suivre, les déterminants de l'usage de l'offre territoriale de soins périnataux. *Recherches familiales*, 12.

Kerbrat-Orrechioni, C. (2005). *Le discours en interaction*. Armand Colin, Paris.

Laforest, M. (2012). De l'intérêt d'articuler les dimensions discursives et interactionnelles de la conversation. Le cas d'une profession en voie de légitimation. *Langue française*, 175, 91–109.

Lécossais, S. (2017). Les mots de la grossesse. *Études de communication*, 48, 155–175.

Moirand, S. (2007). *Les discours de la presse quotidienne. Observer, analyser, comprendre*. PUF, Paris.

Quagliariello, C. (2017). Ces hommes qui accouchent avec nous. La pratique de l'accouchement naturel à l'aune du genre. *Nouvelles questions féministes*, 36(1), 82–97.

Roche, E. and Corroy, L. (2023). When the doctor becomes the patient: The relationship between the caregiver and the breast cancer patient in *Demain nous appartient*. In *Patients, Caregivers and Doctors: Devices, Issues and Representations*, Corroy, L. and Chauzal-Larguier, C. (eds). ISTE Ltd, London, and John Wiley & Sons, New York.

Saint Amant, S. (2015). Naît-on encore ? Réflexions sur la production médicale de l'accouchement. *Recherches familiales*, 12, 9–25.

Schantz, C., Rozée, V., Molinier, P. (2021). Introduction. Les violences obstétricales, un nouvel axe de recherche pour les études de genre, un nouveau défi pour le soin et la société. *Cahiers du Genre*, 71(2), 5–24.

Sen, A. (2000). *Repenser l'inégalité*. Le Seuil, Paris.

Yamgnane, A. (2018). Une approche relationnelle de l'accouchement. *Travail, genre et sociétés*, 39(1), 187–192.

6

Caregivers in the Media: What is the Legitimacy in Their Expertise?

6.1. Introduction

Today, the subject of the health expert in the media spontaneously brings to mind numerous figures, such as researchers, doctors and journalists specializing in health issues, among others. However, from this list, the caregiver is absent.

According to article L. 113-1-3 of the French law on adapting society to aging of December 29, 2015:

> A caregiver of an elderly person is often thought to be their spouse, their partner, including from a civil union, a parent or friend (i.e. family caregivers), a person living with them, or someone with a close and stable relationship to the elderly person, who regularly helps them in a non-professional capacity to carry out all or part of their daily activities.

However, academics and professionals as caregivers alike make extensive reference to the caregiver's expertise (Chamaz 2000; Akrich and Rabeharisoa 2012; Renaud et al. 2019), but are careful to delimit the scope and to formulate a few warnings with regard to its attempts at popularization (Noël-Hureaux 2010). While complimentary to medical/scientific expertise (McClean and Shaw 2005; Grimaldi 2010; Massé 2012; Salman and Topçu

---

Chapter written by Christelle CHAUZAL-LARGUIER and Alexis MEYER.

2015), the expertise of caregivers can be described as "lay", following the example of that of the patient. Not acquired through academic training (Akrich and Rabeharisoa 2012; Salman and Topçu 2015), experiential expertise is gained through lived experience and repeatedly executing multiple tasks for the cared-for person. It is largely based on someone's experiential knowledge of their own situation (Simon et al. 2020) recognized in a care pathway (Cartron et al. 2021), based on the tripartite relationship between patient, carer and family carer, and can be used to provide answers to general problems.

While there is extensive academic research on family that covers many fields (Bloch 2012), it is regrettable that caregiver's expertise in the media remains largely unexplored. Media on caregiving is, generally speaking, made for caregivers and not supported by caregivers themselves (Chauzal-Larguier and Rouquette 2017). This kind of media is mainly published on websites of caregiver associations and for-profit organizations and takes an informational approach (Romeyer 2018). According to caregiver associations, "the voice of caregivers is not very audible" (Leduc and Jung 2012, p. 19). As a result, spokespeople for caregiver associations and the state have been working to communicate and occupy the media sphere to bring caregiving into the public consciousness (as of 2021, 51% of people surveyed knew the term "caregiver," compared with 28% in 2015)[1].

The caregiver thus finds themselves in the position of the receiver, rather than the sender, in the linear model of communication. In everyday life, the caregiver is a shadow actor (Guérin 2012), which seems to be confirmed by the media. As a result, a spiral of silence begins: the caregiver communicates little or not at all, falling into oblivion. This is followed by low media coverage and fewer opportunities to express themselves. The question also arises as to the willingness to give caregivers visibility by giving them a voice. Caregivers still suffer from a "denial of recognition" (Charlier 2018) on the grounds that they are holders of lay expertise. In the end, the question arises as to the legitimacy of this expert in the media. Florence Leduc, former president of the *Association française des aidants* (the French Association of Caregivers), admits that: "Acknowledging the expertise of family caregivers is as essential as it is delicate. It is about highlighting and

1 Data from the *Baromètre des aidants* 2021 – April Foundation, Institut BVA/bva Xsight.

valuing what it is, without confining, rigidifying and ultimately mixing everything up"[2].

The aim of this research project is to provide answers to the following question: How is the expertise of family caregivers mobilized in the media and to what extent is it recognized as legitimate?

Our exploratory study is qualitative in nature (Miles and Huberman 2003) and combines a dual methodological approach. The first involves the study of the discourse of three caregivers, who meet the definition of expert caregivers with both experiential and more technical collective knowledge (see Table 6.1). Frequently, the caregivers interviewed recount their personal experiences – in other words, they testify. However, as we will see later, experience should not be confused with experiential knowledge. This led us to exclude many caregivers, mentioned in press articles or on social networks discussing their individual experience, from our study.

Caregivers in the media	Case presentation	Case reference
Christophe Germain	He benefitted from 170 days' paid leave from his colleagues at the Badoit company in Saint-Galmier (42) to support his son Mathys, who was diagnosed with liver cancer in 2009. He was behind the law on donating working time reduction days (no. 2014-459).	A
Christophe Grosjean	His daughter suffers from a rare disease. His police colleagues wanted to give him some time off, but his superiors refused. He was behind the decree in the civil service sector (decree no. 2015-580) and military (decree no. 2015-573).	B
Sabrina Deliry	Caregiver to her mother, now in a residential home. Co-founder of the *Cercle des proches aidants en Ehpad* (CPAE, Circle of Caregivers in Nursing Homes) and the *Observatoire du grand âge* (OGRA, Old Age Observatory).	C

Table 6.1. *Corpus from the study of three cases of caregivers covered in the media*

Our analysis focuses on how the media presents and organizes the lay expertise of caregivers. We will examine three themes: the form and content

2 Leduc, F. (2019). Lumière sur l'expertise des proches aidants [Online]. Available at: https://www.aidonslesnotre.fr/le-role-delaidant/lumiere-sur-lexpertise-des-proches-aidants/.

of these discourses, and the communication media mobilized. Details of each are given in Table 6.2.

Themes	Subtopics
Analysis of communication form	What place is given to the voice of caregivers in the media (quotes from caregivers, presentation, etc.)? What visual representations of caregivers are present (video, photo, etc.)? Is the caregiver the only person in the communication (function of other people, form of presence)? What place is given to caregiver's expertise (references)?
Analysis of discourse types	This analysis focuses on the existence and content of the various discourses: testimonial discourse, informational discourse on caregiving, discourse popularization and expert discourse.
Analysis of communication materials	This study focuses on the various communication media available to caregivers (Internet, social networks, print media, TV, radio).

Table 6.2. *List of content analysis criteria of cases studied*

The second half of our study analyzes the perspectives of 10 people interviewed from different sectors (associations, politics, journalism) related to aid/care provision (Table 6.3) between 2017 and 2022, which lasted from 45 minutes to 1 hour 30 minutes. Many have had, or are having, an unmediated experience. The aim here was to discuss the legitimacy of the caregivers' lay expertise. We combined the interview results with a study of online content and actor logics, in order to better understand the way in which lay expertise of caregivers is mobilized in the media as well as the legitimacy of this expertise.

In the first part of this chapter, we will look at the lay expertise of caregivers in the media. Indeed, caregivers have expertise to bring to the media, and we will see what their current place is within it. In the second part, we will discuss the legitimacy of their expertise. Because it is not recognized by the media, the caregiver's expertise is not very visible to the general public, even though it is very real.

Roles	Interview reference
Former caregiver and president of a caregiver association	Interview 1
Former caregiver and president of a national association for caregivers and patients	Interview 2
Former caregiver and president of the departmental section (i.e. county branch) of a patients' association	Interview 3
Former head of the local chapter of a patients' association	Interview 4
General delegate of a national caregivers' collective	Interview 5
Responsible for listening and providing information on a telephone platform for caregivers	Interview 6
Project manager for a national event for caregivers	Interview 7
Caregiver	Interview 8
Journalist for a regional daily newspaper	Interview 9
Vice-president of a company that granted paid-leave to an employee who was a caregiver	Interview 10

Table 6.3. *Corpus of interviewees*

6.2. Caregivers and their lay expertise in the media

6.2.1. *Lay experiential expertise*

Testimony is a method of gathering information that is widely used in the social sciences, and whose relevance is indisputable. However, testimony, or in other words, the sharing of personal experience, does not qualify as expertise. Experiential expertise goes further: it combines experience with lay knowledge, derived from experience, the frequency of which leads us to believe that it can be generalized, thus transforming experiential knowledge.

The term "expert caregiver" is inspired by the expert patient since both possess similar (or at least complementary) forms of experiential knowledge. According to the definition accepted by the European Organisation for Rare Diseases (EURORDIS) and the European Medicines Agency (EMA), an expert patient "is someone suffering from a chronic health condition who has developed a detailed knowledge of their condition over time and thus possesses genuine expertise in the day-to-day experience of a pathology or physical limitation linked to their condition". They acquire "experiential knowledge (stemming from knowledge of the disease in vivo)" (Boudier et al. 2012, p. 19) through new information and communication technologies and therapeutic education programs for caregivers (Tourette-Turgis 2015). An expert patient is first and foremost a "peer helper" for direct exchanges and experience-sharing with patients and their loved ones, whatever the form.

The notion of the expert caregiver was introduced by Nolan and Keady (2001). In their view, we need to move beyond the "person-centered model of care", which is implicitly individualistic, towards a model of "care centered on the relationship between the carer and the patient", which fully accounts for the dynamic relations between all parties involved. "I met people who helped me, and I was able to take part in a caregiver training course, which opened my eyes" (Interview 3, 2022).

While the notion of the expert has been the subject of a large amount of scholarship, that of the expert caregiver remains little explored and little known, even though it is used both by academics and by caregivers themselves (Roumanoff 2017). Coudin and Mollard (2011, p. 364) explain that "caregivers need to be recognized in their role as caregivers. To do so, he or she must obtain the skills, know-how and resources needed to provide good-quality care, without endangering their own health". They need to be trained and given the necessary resources (Renaud et al. 2019, p. 12), which is essential for acquiring knowledge:

> It is very important for the caregiver to have training. At the beginning, training courses are about getting to the bottom of things and gradually moving towards the future. It's about trying to wake up caregivers and getting them to learn about situations under a little less stress (Interview 3, 2022).

The notion of experiential knowledge was introduced by Borkman (1976). Although experiential knowledge is seen as a "polysemous, catch-all concept" (Hejoaka et al. 2019), it can be defined as knowledge that is "individual, pragmatic, situated in the 'here and now', and holistic, based on shared/collective experience/s" (Hejoaka et al. 2019). It is "fundamental to recognize experiential knowledge as a genuine, respectable and useful type of knowledge" (Hautefeuille 2021, p. 6). Experiential knowledge involves a long temporal approach and introduces the concept of learning the status of the caregiver removed from any state of spontaneity, but rather over time: "[The caregiver] is obliged to learn as they go, because the person being cared for cannot change their behavior" (Interview 8, 2022).

The caregiver is thus able to "position themselves as a consultant with experiential knowledge" (Champion and Gilbert 2022, p. 2) and the ability to address the technical aspects of health conditions, as shown by the following comments made by a former caregiver about Lewy body disease:

> It's an illness with extremely large fluctuations even within the same day, and so the person being cared for gets completely panicked by these changes in their mental state that they can't control by mood alone, changes to their physical abilities, and hallucinations that are basically permanent, and will come, and then a create real paranoia. (Interview 8, 2022)

Far from being testimonial, such a discourse is based on relative knowledge of the disease and demonstrates the caregiver's lay expertise on the subject, which goes beyond just experience.

Experiential expertise has this capacity to become public and collective (Clause-Verdreau 2019) and "translates into a competence to mobilize experiential knowledge to provide answers to problems formulated in general or specific terms" (Akrich and Rabeharisoa 2012, p. 70). Indeed, "the very success of the term 'caregiver(s)', which is now standard, testifies to this process of generalization to the point of becoming a public cause" (Chanial and Gaglio 2013, p. 123):

> We need to recognize that caregivers of elderly and disabled people are experts, and above all take advantage of their expertise to improve existing schemes and services and devise new ones. (Interview 8, 2022)

The caregiver can then take part in an approach to expertise which, as Clause-Verdreau (2020, p. 150) notes, can be called "co-expertise." After all, the caregiver's expertise is predominantly based on their relationship with the person being cared for.

6.2.2. *Demonstrative relevance in the media space*

Today, caregivers mobilize a variety of communication media and reinforce their media presence by being simultaneously present on social networks, radio, television and in the local and national press. The reasoning for this media coverage by caregivers is that "communication tools complement each other. There's a complementarity between the Internet and social networks" (Interview 7, 2017) or even "a synergy. The Internet is used for more official communication, and social networks when we want to publicize an event. From now on, we need to mobilize the whole" (Interview 1, 2017). The Internet provides us with information, while social media creates interactivity. As such, caregivers create social media accounts specifically for this reason.

The content of the discourse does not center on a personal situation (e.g. "I had an accident and I couldn't look after my mom anymore, who has all her wits about her", Case C, *Télématin*, 2022), and it therefore cannot be called testimonial. On the contrary, it can be used to enhance an initial collective, as in the case of paid leave, for example: "They mustn't minimize their efforts, because what they've done is extraordinary. I didn't ask them to do anything, they suggested it. It's their law too" (Case A, *France Bleu*, 2014). The mediatized can involve another person (colleague, husband/wife), either directly by having them intervene when they speak in the media or through thought:

> I was a caregiver for my wife whilst she was sick until her death in 2016. We told ourselves that we had to do something to make this disease better known. (Interview 2, 2021)

The latter intervened to provide additional information, as the mother of the person being helped does in Case B: "I know that the administration is a big machine. But even within it, we expect one person to show humanity and unblock things" (Case B, BFM, 2014). Interviews may or may not be accompanied by photographs of the caregiver, people from the family or professional circle, or, more rarely, the person being cared for (deceased or not).

For caregivers, communicating their presence in the media "is about making known what exists and making caregivers known" (Interview 6, 2017). Today, traditional and digital media can serve as a sounding board for the discourse of caregivers and their commitments. Easier access to information and the multiplicity of sources via new information technologies (Broom 2005), changes in legislation, the structuring of the associative medium linked to caregiving, the growing interest in these issues in the public arena open up to the caregiver the path taken by patients before them. Noël-Hureaux (2010) describes this as "empowerment". As such, caregivers can move towards a more active position in the media: "Some want to stay silent, whereas others don't – they want to promote their work" (Interview 9, 2016).

Above all, the caregiver's media presence allows them to wage another fight that stems from their personal experience as a carer, but on behalf of the majority of caregivers: "It's the result of my son's ongoing battle" (Case A, RTL, 2012). This battle aims to bring the various failings into the public arena, whether they relate to the legal provisions in force ("I wrote to my superiors last July to find out what they could do to help me. I got no reply for seven months" (Case B, *L'Est républicain*, 2014)); economic measures ("But in these cases, if you take a month's leave, the pay comes to 900 euros" (Case A, France TV info, 2014)); or linked to dysfunctions existing in healthcare structures such as care homes ("The lie exists. The danger has been there from the start. We want to know why and who made these criminal decisions"; "We've been robbed of our last moments with our loved ones" (Case C, France 3 région; France TV info, 2020)).

The discourse of the caregiver in the media is clearly focused on the search for solutions, be they legislative or financial advancements, recognition of the status of caregiver, visiting rights, etc. For example, consider this statement from Case A: "It is a great personal satisfaction that my son's struggle is the origin of this bill" (Case A, *Le Monde*, 2012). The aim of this statement is to push for the legalization of existing practices to benefit other people: "We are moved by the passing of this bill, which stems from our personal history, for all the parents who will be able to benefit from it" (Case A, France TV info, 2012). In this way, the caregiver's thoughts are reflected in the media in favor of the generalization of a system. It is therefore a discourse of expertise based on the experiential knowledge acquired from the carer's previous experiences. To lend additional weight to their struggle, caregivers can call on the support of professionals who can bring a field of expertise that complements their own.

In two of the three cases studied, the caregiver is supported by a professional, who may also be a political expert (e.g. an MP or a minister) or a healthcare professional (e.g. a doctor), to succeed in co-constructing the figure of the mediated expert caregiver. This support may or may not be requested by the caregiver. In Case A, Germain took the initiative to contact the deputy Paul Salen; in Case B, Grosjean was heard on the radio by Marylise Lebranchu, who was Minister of the Civil Service at the time, and publically lent him her support, bringing his case before the competent authorities. Professionals also express themselves in the media, but rarely alongside the caregiver so as not to confuse or weaken their respective messages, but with a specific aim to be heard: "It took media pressure" (Interview 9, 2016).

Media coverage is limited in time; as we can see in both Cases A and B, once the fight is over, the caregiver fades back into anonymity and disappears from the media sphere. Germain spoke in the media for five years, between taking paid leave in 2009 and the publication in the *Journal officiel* of law no. 2014-459 allowing the donation of days off for a parent of a seriously ill child (2014). Grosjean denounced, in the same way, the limits of a text not applicable in the public service until the publication in the *Journal officiel* of the decree of application to civil public agents (decree no. 2015-580) and military (decree no. 2015-573) for one year (2014–2015). There is a sort of media sanction once the goal is achieved. The caregiver, however, continues to use their platforms on social media. Deliry (Case C) continues to speak out against the conditions of lockdown and life in nursing homes. She is the most publicized caregiver in the long-run because she uses her notoriety to express herself in the media on subjects related to assistance (such as old age, dependency, etc.), which allowed her to access another status, professional this time, as mentioned in Table 6.1. These three cases show that the valorization of experiential knowledge through experiential expertise is possible.

6.3. The legitimacy of caregivers' expertise

6.3.1. *The legitimacy of expertise*

The term "caregiver resource" is used by some hospitals in which "the word 'resource' refers to the idea that the caregiver is seen as a source of information, and can offer another point of view based on their experiences and lived experience" (Champion and Gilbert 2022, p. 3), to the extent that they are considered a "caregiver partner" (Champion and Gilbert 2022, p. 3) and are able to work with medical staff. The caregiver's experiential knowledge can be of interest and use to a wide audience of healthcare professionals and peer helpers, but also – and it is something we do not always think about it – the general public, who can be reached through the media. Yet experiential expertise of caregivers, in both cases, needs to find its place.

Numerous research studies highlight how difficult it is for expert patients and expert caregivers to be recognized and accepted (Fainzang 2010; Friconneau et al. 2020). Clause-Verdreau (2020, p. 149) stresses the ambivalence that surrounds recognizing caregiver's expertise, as it can be seen as a kind of "profanation" of the scientific expertise of the medical profession, while at the same time being both legitimate and valid in the face of scientific expertise:

> Given that people who work with disabled people are full-time caregivers, their expertise could be very useful in supporting the department's policy in favor of caregivers. (Case 8, 2022)

Ultimately, we can see that the question of the caregiver's legitimacy to intervene on health issues remains unresolved. But why is this? Suchman (1995, p. 574) defines legitimacy as a "generalized perception or assumption that an entity's actions are desirable and appropriate within a socially constructed system of norms, values, beliefs and definitions". The caregiver is recognized as having legitimacy to communicate in specific cases: "An initiative, to talk about daily life, to ask for public assistance" (Interview 5, 2022).

For associative players, this is also tied to the profile of family carers. For example, it would be useful to distinguish between those who help a disabled person and those who support a dependent elderly person, as the length of the caregiving period varies, and this influences the desire, or even the need, to maintain some form of commitment. In the first case, "involvement goes beyond the child's disappearance. Parents continue to get involved. It's common. They make it their duty to continue". However, in the second case, when the person being cared for dies, "the carer disappears from the social field" (Interview 1, 2017). This is also due to the fact that "former caregivers now have more time and desire to share their experiences" (Interview 3, 2022).

And yet, especially at the local level, a caregiver seeks help and support from a disease-specific association (Parkinson's, Alzheimer's, etc.), as those dedicated to caregivers rarely have local branches. When the period of assistance comes to an end, many caregivers wish to maintain a connection with the association that provided them with information and support by taking on greater responsibilities within the association. This explains how, for example, a former caregiver can become head of a departmental branch of a national association. Indeed, many caregivers' associations "operate thanks to volunteers" (Interview 4, 2017). This raises the question of both the scope of the caregiver's expertise and its legitimacy in the media. Within their discourse the visions of the caregiver and the local association leader complement each other, as the former provides testimony ("When I saw people holding hands in the street, I cried, because I couldn't do it anymore" (Interview 3, 2022)) and knowledge on the subject, while the latter requires a different level of analysis and a certain distance, a sense of perspective:

> You should know that the caregiver is the beacon of light for the patient, who clings to him, […] neuro-progressive diseases are a prison for the sick. (Interview 3, 2022)

The legitimacy of caregivers' expertise is subject to debate between healthcare professionals and associations alike. They warn that the caregiver can claim to be an expert on a disease, as illustrated by an article co-authored by a healthcare professional and a member of an Alzheimer's foundation (Selmès and Derouesné 2006). This distinction is, in fact, fundamental. As the *Association française des aidants* warns, "expert does not mean professional, and it would be extremely dangerous to attribute to caregivers roles that they should not be invested in and thus contribute to a mixing of genres that would in no way strengthen the role and place of the caregiver with regard to both the person he or she supports and society" (Leduc and Jung 2012, p. 21). The message is clear: if caregivers are to have their expertise recognized, they must rightly remain confined to the field of the layperson. The three cases studied in section 6.1 are no exception. The associations fear that caregivers, by expressing themselves individually, may blur the messages. The caregiver is not a professional in communication and may find themselves little or poorly prepared (Leduc et al. 2013) and prey to strong emotions (Mallon and Le Bihan-Youinou 2017).

The question of the legitimacy of caregivers to intervene in the media implicitly raises that of the popularization of discourse. Finally, the caregiver's expertise is recognized more within associations and hospitals – i.e. in fairly restricted spheres and not in the media, a very broad sphere par excellence, and where they are not considered legitimate to share their experiential expertise. The expertise of the caregiver therefore encounters difficulties in getting past the stage of sharing with the general public.

6.3.2. *Non-media coverage of the caregiver's expertise*

Today, the topic of family caregivers is subject to more media coverage than in the past, which has helped combat the public's lack of awareness of them: "We're a topic that's more in the spotlight" (Interview 1, 2017). If the caregiver has become known in the media, this is not necessarily by their own doing, but, as we have said, a result of the work of associations and the state. The caregiver is in fact reluctant to self-publicize and remains focused on their experience as a caregiver:

> They are isolated, they are entirely focused on helping those they care for. Caregivers are often withdrawn from the care recipient and from themselves. (Case 3, 2022)

Associations have noted that the topic of family caregivers is attracting a lot of media attention:

> The media have turned it into something of a chestnut. We used to have an annual interest, but now there's a real interest. Rarely does a fortnight go by without a media outlet contacting us. Society at large is interested in the topic. (Interview 1, 2017)

However, journalists are more interested in the empathy that the caregiving situation generates than in caregivers' expertise:

> It's information in its own right, and what's more, it's information that people like to read. There's empathy for these stories. (Interview 9, 2016)

But the topic of caregivers can also lead the journalist to engage in a more amoral approach: "On the one hand, there are those concerned with factual information, and on the other, those looking for a front page story"

(Interview 10, 2016). This kind of downward spiral can lead caregivers to fear a certain kind of voyeurism: "She doesn't want to talk about it. She has a serious family problem, she doesn't want to be bothered with it" (Case 10, 2016).

As a result, journalistic articles focus on two key elements: a context ("We have, as a local newspaper, a proximity to readers" (Interview 9, 2016)) and a caregiver's testimony. According to the journalist interviewed, interest is circumscribed to the local field only ("It's reported on the local page only" (Interview 9, 2016)) and a caregiver testimonial without expertise is expected.

Today, the caregiver as a health expert is not a figure that exists in the media: the caregiver's expertise is not sought. Yet, media coverage of caregivers requires them to be recognized by the media. The expert caregiver, through their lay expertise, does not intend to substitute the figure of the doctor and their scientific expertise. Rather, by sharing their expertise in the media, the caregiver hopes to contribute to a better knowledge of the patient with a range of other actors whose coordination they ensure at home (Jarrossay and Paternostre 2020), for better monitoring of nursing and household care, for example, and to share their experiential knowledge with a broad target audience, the general public. This suggests a kind of "media reluctance" among caregivers, when collaborating with a team of healthcare professionals in drawing up a care protocol. "To free oneself from this power struggle is to liberate oneself, to emancipate oneself from the representations surrounding medical knowledge, in order to give equivalent, or even greater, value to experiential knowledge" (Champion and Gilbert 2022, p. 7). However, Balcou-Debussche (2006) points out that lay knowledge must have its place alongside medical discourse, as it highlights different aspects of the disease. In reality, this is not so obvious.

6.4. Conclusion

This research provides some answers to the question of the mediatization of the caregiver, their expertise, and legitimacy. It shows that caregivers have lay expertise that can be mobilized in the media, which can serve as a sounding board. Caregiver expertise as expressed in the media has evolved in both form and content. The individual testimonial has enabled experiential knowledge to be considered expertise. Yet, few caregivers share this experiential experience in the media, and it remains circumstantial to specific moments and sought-after little by the media. The legitimacy of their expertise is debated, for want of real recognition. Today, if the caregiver is covered by the media, and if the expert caregiver exists, their expertise is not publicized.

The research perspectives are threefold. Firstly, at the conceptual level, a communication approach to the caregiver is envisaged through a reflection on the place of the caregiver in the communication strategy on caregiving, authorizing a move from the concept of expert caregiver to collective expertise and questioning the legitimacy of the caregiver in this communication. Secondly, at another level, it is appropriate to consider expertise through the prism of its recognition. Indeed, as underlined by Leduc, the former president of the *Association française des aidants* (Leduc 2019), the question of recognizing the caregiver's expertise raises other questions: "What recognition is society ready to grant this expertise? Is it a matter of collectively relying on it? To develop it and mobilize it to save money? To move towards more family solidarity and less national solidarity?" The lay expertise of the caregiver must find its rightful place in the media, and the contours of the latter are still partially to be defined. Third, at the methodological level, a new phase of this work has begun, which involves continuing to interview those involved in caregiving, as well as examining the network of actors around the caregiver (such as carer associations, medical professionals, policymakers, public organizations, structures welcoming caregivers, etc.). The goal is to better understand how the relevance of the caregiver's expertise is viewed in the media.

Even today, the place that could be given in the media to the caregiver as a lay expert has yet to be won. This calls on the researcher to prepare the caregiver in advance, both to help the media discover the content of this lay expertise, so as to arouse their interest, and to give the caregiver the keys to promoting their lay expertise in the media.

6.5. References

Akrich, M. and Rabeharisoa, V. (2012). L'expertise profane dans les associations de patients, un outil de démocratie sanitaire. *Santé Publique*, 24(1), 69–74.

Balcou-Debussche, M. (2006). *L'éducation des maladies chroniques*. Les éditions des archives contemporaines, Paris.

Bloch, M.A. (2012). Les aidants et l'émergence d'un nouveau champ de recherche interdisciplinaire. *Vie sociale*, 4, 11–29.

Borkman, T. (1976). Experiential knowledge: A new concept for the analysis of self-help groups. *Social Service Review*, 50(3), 445–456.

Boudier, F., Bensebaa, F., Jablanczy, A. (2012). L'émergence du patient-expert : une perturbation innovante. *Innovations*, 39(3), 13–25.

Broom, A. (2005). Medical specialist' accounts of the impact of the internet on the doctor/patient relationship. *Health*, 9(3), 319–333.

Cartron, E., Lefebvre, S., Jovic, L. (2021). Le savoir expérientiel : exploration épistémologique d'une expression répandue dans le domaine de la santé. *Recherche en soins infirmiers*, 144, 76–86.

Chamaz, K. (2000). Experiencing chronic illness. In *The Handbook of Social Studies in Health and Medicine*, Albrecht, G.L., Fitzpatrick, R., Scrimshaw, S.C. (eds). Sage, London.

Champion, S. and Gilbert, J.P. (2022). Identité et reconnaissance du savoir expérientiel de l'aidant-ressource. *Santé Éducation*, 32 [Online]. Available at: https://www.afdet.net/wp-content/uploads/2022/05/Article-Aidant-ressource.pdf.

Chanial, P. and Gaglio, G. (2013). Aidons les aidants. Une initiative mutualiste face au marché de la dépendance. *Revue du MAUSS*, 41, 121–139.

Charlier, E. (2018). Aidants proches : une reconnaissance en demi-teinte ? *La Revue Nouvelle*, 4, 59–64.

Chauzal-Larguier, C. and Rouquette, S. (2017). Médias sociaux et associations d'aidants familiaux. Risques ou opportunités ? *Les cahiers du numérique*, 13(2), 75–104.

Clause-Verdreau, A.C. (2020). Reconnaître les expériences et les expertises. Retour sur les journées "Ethique, Alzheimer et maladies neuro-évolutives". *Revue française d'éthique appliquée*, 1(9), 144–151.

Coudin, G. and Mollard, J. (2011). Être aidant de malade Alzheimer : difficultés, stratégies de faire face et gratifications. *Gériatrie et psychologie neuropsychiatrie du vieillissement*, 9(3), 363–378.

Fainzang, S. (2010). Le pouvoir du patient face au médecin : entre expérience, compétence et savoir. *Pratiques de formation/Analyses*, 57, 123–134.

Friconneau, M., Archer, A., Malaterre, J., Salama, F., Ouillade, M.C. (2020). Le patient-expert. *Médecine/sciences*, 36(2), 62–64.

Grimaldi, A. (2010). Les différents habits de l'"expert profane". *Les tribunes de la santé*, 2(27), 91–100.

Guerin, S. (2012). Les aidants, cœur du système social. *Revue Projet*, 1(326), 47–54.

Hautefeuille, M. (2021). Médiateur de santé publique, médiateur santé pair, pair-aidant, patient expert ? Éditorial. *Psychotropes*, 27(1/2), 5–9.

Hejoaka, F., Simon, E., Halloy, A., Arborio, S. (2019). Définir les savoirs expérientiels en santé : une revue de la littérature en sciences humaines et sociales. *Questions de communication*, 49–74.

Jarrossay, E. and Paternostre, B. (2020). Perception par les proches aidants de leurs rôles et fonctions face aux douleurs cancéreuses en situation palliative spécifique ou symptomatique au domicile. *Médecine Palliative*, 19(4), 207–213.

Le Pen, C. (2009). "Patient" ou "personne malade" ? *Revue économique*, 60(2), 257–272.

Leduc, F. (2019). Lumière sur l'expertise des proches aidants ! *Aidons les nôtres* [Online]. Available at: https://www.aidonslesnotres.fr/le-role-de-laidant/lumiere-sur-lexpertise-des-proches-aidants/?pdf=1446.

Leduc, F. and Jung, E. (2012). Un lobby des aidants est-il possible ? *Documents Cleirppa*, 47, 19.

Leduc, F., Jung, E., Lozac'h, C. (2013). Former les aidants : comment ? Pourquoi ? Pour quoi faire ? *Gérontologie et société*, 36(147), 189–198.

Mallon, I. and Le Bihan-Youinou, B. (2017). Le poids des émotions. Une réflexion sur les variations de l'intensité de l'(entr)aide familiale auprès de proches dépendants. *Sociologie*, 8(2), 121–138.

Massé, R. (2012). Expertises éthiques savantes et profanes en santé publique : défis et enjeux pour une éthique de la discussion. *Santé Publique*, 24(1), 49–61.

McClean, S. and Shaw, A. (2005). From schism to continuum? The problematic relationship between expert and lay knowledge – An exploratory conceptual synthesis of two qualitative studies. *Qualitative Health Research*, 15(6), 729–749.

Miles, B.M. and Huberman, A.M. (2003). *Analyse des données qualitatives*. De Boeck, Brussels.

Noel-Hureaux, E. (2010). Quels savoirs "en jeu" (enjeux) autour de la maladie chronique ? *Pratiques de formation/Analyses*, 58(59), 111–124.

Nolan, M. and Keady, J. (2001). Working with careers. In *Handbook of Dementia Care*, Cantley, C. (ed.). Open University Press, Milton Keynes.

Renaud, J., Nour, M., Houssin, R., Gerdoni, M. (2019). Rôle de l'aidant d'une personne atteinte de la maladie d'Alzheimer ou apparentée, à l'ère du numérique. *La Revue de Gériatrie*, 44(4), 227–240.

Romeyer, H. (2018). TIC et santé : entre information médicale et information de santé. *TIC & Société*, 2(1), 27–44.

Roumanoff, C. (2017). *Alzheimer : accompagner ceux qu'on aime (et les autres)*. Librio, Paris.

Salman, S. and Topçu, S. (2015). Expertise profane. In *Dictionnaire critique de l'expertise. Santé, travail, environnement*, Henry, E., Gilbert, C., Jouzel, J.N., Marichalar, P. (eds). Presses de Sciences Po, Paris.

Selmes, J. and Derouesné, C. (2006). Maladie d'Alzheimer : cinq protagonistes en quête d'identité. *Médecine*, 2(7), 307–308.

Simon, E., Arborio, S., Halloy, A., Hejoaka, F. (eds) (2020). *Les savoirs expérientiels en santé. Fondements épistémologiques et enjeux identitaires*. Presses universitaires de Lorraine, Nancy.

Suchman, M.C. (1995). Managing legitimacy: Strategic and institutional approaches. *Academy of Management Review*, 20(3), 571–610.

Tattersall, R.L. (2002). The expert patient: A new approach to chronic disease management for the twenty-first century. *Clinical Medicine*, 2(3), 227–229. doi: 10.7861/clinmedicine.2-3-227.

Tourette-Turgis, C. (2015). *L'education thérapeutique du patient : la maladie comme occasion d'apprentissage*. De Boeck, Brussels.

7

The Long Covid Patient: Legitimizing Patient Experience

7.1. Introduction

The symptoms associated with Covid-19 infection were initially understood in their acute form. But many patients (an estimated one in ten) report symptoms that persist beyond three weeks (post-acute symptoms) or even beyond 12 weeks (chronic symptoms). Post-acute and chronic symptoms have been grouped together under the term "long Covid", which was coined by the patients themselves (Perego et al. 2020) to capture what they experienced and continue to experience. These patients now have a name for their altered state of health, which makes it visible. It is difficult to say exactly how many people have long Covid, as these patients were – and in some cases still are – not identified by doctors, due to the lack of a registry for documenting these cases and the persistent symptoms experienced by patients. In order to make themselves heard, and thereby benefit from care and attention tailored to their unique situation, these patients have organized themselves to take action. Thus, as a result of their collective efforts, patients suffering from persistent Covid symptoms have managed to bring the long Covid pathology into existence in record time, unlike other patient groups (including HIV-positive patients and parents of individuals with autism spectrum disorders, etc.) who worked for years to raise awareness of their situation and have it recognized.

Chapter written by Corinne ROCHETTE.

Established actors have often ignored or misunderstood the contributions of patients and laypersons, which has only intensified patient suffering and societal inequalities (Callard and Perego 2021). Over the last 10 years or so, patient care has taken a new turn: in addition to assessing patient satisfaction, some researchers are now interested in their experiences. Gathering and understanding patient's experiences of an illness not only helps researchers to improve care and personalize treatment paths, but it also contributes to scientific knowledge about the disease's symptoms and effects. The patient experience approach can be particularly useful in the case of new diseases, since they are poorly documented in their emergence phase. Long Covid is one of these. It was the first disease to be "created" (so to speak) by patients (Yong 2020) through digital social networks (Pope 2020)[1] based on lived experience. In February 2021, the World Health Organization (WHO) Regional Director for Europe stated at a press conference, reported in an article in *Le Point* magazine on February 25, 2021, that long Covid is "a clear WHO priority and of the utmost importance. […] All too often, these symptoms come up against disbelief and/or a lack of understanding".

How then, in a context in which medical professionals have the monopoly over medical knowledge and medical action, were patients able to label "long Covid" and have a new pathology recognized? How did they manage to legitimize their action in a context in which the scientific legitimacy of the medical profession remains strong?

To answer these questions, I will draw on research on patient experience and empowerment, as well as the theoretical framework of legitimacy (section 7.2). Using the case study of the French association *ApresJ20*, I intend to respond to Callard and Perego's (2021) call for work that documents patients' contributions to the recognition of long Covid in countries outside of the UK and the USA (see section 7.3). I will add fresh insight to the process of legitimizing long Covid, which serves as a powerful example of how lay knowledge is able to influence the direction of health policy (see section 7.4).

1 See: https://twitter.com/preshitorian/status/1242831605330313216.

7.2. The emergence of legitimate expert knowledge

7.2.1. *From lay knowledge to expertise: the role of empowerment*

Recognition of patients' expertise is the result of a process of slow changes to the traditional dominance of doctors and their medical knowledge. Patient expertise has its roots in the patient experience and the transformation in France of the patient's status. In the 1970s, the patient's illness changed from "object of care" to "subject of care." From the 1970s onwards, patients' associations revolted against the impotence of medicine, including *AIDES* (the first French association to combat HIV) and the *Association française contre les myopathies* (the French Muscular Dystrophy Association) and took on the unprecedented role of transmitting knowledge. In France, this hitherto unprecedented involvement of patients led to the creation of the March 4, 2002 law on "patients' rights" and remains a unique example of the co-creation of a legislative text. These developments in the second half of the 20th century formed the foundation for institutional and community empowerment (Anderson and Funnell 2010), and the opening up of healthcare organization governance to their patients.

At the same time, increasingly easy access to medical information and the chronicization of numerous pathologies have resulted in individual empowerment. The patient educates themselves about health, even though there is much to learn. They learn to self-manage their symptoms and their state of health. They develop their literacy (Berkman et al. 2010; Osborne 2012; Kickbusch et al. 2013; Košir and Sørensen 2022) and their ability to navigate (Freeman and Rodriguez 2011; Freeman 2012; Broeckaert and Challacombe 2014) in the health system. For some, we could even say that they become somewhat professional. Empowerment therefore has both an individual and a collective dimension.

Empowerment begins with a process of "individual emancipation that is rooted in changes in the social, economic, and political structures of society" (Duvall 1999, p. 209). It goes hand in hand with the acquisition of knowledge and skills. For Rappaport (1987), empowerment is both a means and an end. They state that the overall aim of empowerment is to liberate minority social groups by relying on collectives formed around the deployment of an identity, or the promotion or assertion of a cause: "Thus, empowerment is not only an individual psychological construct, but is also organizational, political, sociological, etc." (Rappaport 1987, p. 130). Research into patient empowerment (Holmström and Röing 2010; Castro et al. 2016), patient experience (Wolf and Jason 2014) and patient expertise (Boudier et al. 2012) all highlight that it is the patient's possession of certain knowledge that enables them to become more active and involved in their own health and, more broadly, to contribute to the development of the changing face of the healthcare system and patient care. The patient's new role counterbalances the paternalistic approach that has long prevailed in the medical world (Staples 1990).

Empowerment is at the heart of research into health literacy (Sørensen et al. 2012) – a concept widely promoted by WHO, and around which a stream of research has developed (Sørensen et al. 2012). Health literacy has been conceptualized as a set of capabilities that are partly knowledge-based. It is context-specific and influenced by interactions and health structures (Nutbeam 2008). There are many definitions of health literacy, but we can identify four key themes:

- accessing/obtaining relevant health information;
- understanding relevant health information;
- processing/appraising relevant health information;
- applying/using relevant health information (Nutbeam 1999; Sørensen et al. 2012; Osborne et al. 2013).

The patient becomes a resource not only for their own benefit, but also for that of the collective. They gradually acquire expert status through their ability to mobilize their experiences and demonstrate reflexivity. In this way, the individual patient's power is strengthened by becoming collective power through the creation and sharing of knowledge (Rabeharisoa and Callon 2002), with patients even playing an active role in the direction of research. Researchers see experience as a multidimensional construct with cognitive, emotional, social, sensory and behavioral (including physical behavior) dimensions (Hirschman and Holbrook 1982; Lemon and Verhoef 2016).

Empowerment is both a process and a result. On the one hand, it is a process that refers to the patient's ability to develop in order to think critically and act autonomously. On the other hand, it is also a result that can be measured through the number of decisions taken independently. Most studies have explored the link between empowerment and experience, without actually referring (explicitly?) to expertise and putting these two notions into perspective. Experience and expertise are two very different notions, which raises the question: At what point does experience become expertise?

Experience does not necessarily lead to expertise; to do so, it requires critical distance and some literacy. Patient knowledge is individual and pragmatic, rather than theoretical and scientific. It is local and anchored in the moment (i.e. the here and now) and is also holistic, since it concerns a phenomenon as a whole and in a non-professional way (Klein 2014). Therefore, it is clear that experience does not necessarily become expertise, except when it has been the subject of reflective work. It is then envisaged and recognized by others as a legitimate and valid resource on which to base decisions and actions.

Expertise can be understood in two ways. The first refers to the *expertus*, that is someone who has proven themselves and acquired great skill and know-how in a profession or discipline through extensive experience. This makes them an "expert in" the field in question. The second approach refers to the technical dimension of expertise, i.e. the professional specialist who has been approved by a body, such as a court. Here, the expert is "empowered by [the] law" to analyze, evaluate, give their opinion and make a decisive judgment on the situation at hand. Ultimately, however, the expert is the one who is able to mobilize and use experiential knowledge to solve other people's problems and influence their environment. They acquire legitimacy through interaction and reflexivity, i.e. by testing their knowledge in real-life situations (Dewey 2004). It is only recently that this notion of the expert has been used to describe patients who are recognized as able to understand and deal with their illness, have demonstrated reflexivity and can provide answers in a reasoned and distanced way to questions from others. It is with this objective in mind that new organizational forms such as patient universities[2] and university training courses (expert patient university diploma) have emerged and are described by their promoters as socially innovative.

2 "The Université des Patients-Sorbonne, founded in 2010 [...] is an innovative university that offers degree courses for people living with an illness who wish to transform their lived experience of illness into expertise that benefits the community". See: https://universitedespatients-sorbonne.fr/.

The literature has highlighted several types of patient expertise according to the following factors: the nature of patient expertise (such as experiential expertise and technical expertise); its positioning (e.g. counter-expertise, complementary expertise and conforming expertise) and finally, its direction (e.g. endo-expertise, which is expertise turned towards oneself, and exo-expertise, which is turned towards others) (Klein 2014). Over the past 10 years, as patient expertise has been afforded more legitimacy, this has brought about expressions such as patient expert, patient partner, patient trainer, etc. (Flora 2013), and models such as those designed to represent this very particular empowerment (e.g. the Montreal model by Pomey et al. (2015)). This seems to mark a paradigmatic shift in the medical world and, more broadly, in how health is understood. Thus, healthcare systems must no longer *act on behalf of* patients but must act *with* them, drawing on patients' experience (Wolf et al. 2014). The Covid-19 pandemic is a particularly original example of the affirmation of the patient experience and the biopolitical stakes of health and illness (Dahl Rendtorff 2021) in an unfamiliar situation (initially marked by a lack of scientific data) for the medical profession. Indeed, how, in a context of lack of knowledge on the clinical effects of the coronavirus, did the "new disease" long Covid emerge in France from the action of patients? And how is this "new disease" legitimized?

7.2.2. Legitimizing lay knowledge

Legitimacy is a complex philosophical and sociological concept rooted in Max Weber's work on the sources of power and authority (Cotterrell 1997; Kauffmann 2014). Since Weber, the concept has been widely mobilized by researchers in sociology and organizational management (Suchman 1995; Deephouse and Suchman 2008; Suddaby 2010; Deephouse et al. 2017), to explore the normative and cognitive forces that constrain, construct and reinforce organizations. Suchman (1995) defines legitimacy as an evolving status granted by stakeholders to varying degrees, depending on the organization's ability to convince that the way it operates meets the criteria of their social systems.

Legitimacy has several dimensions. The first is conformity with the law: the term "legitimacy" comes from the Latin word *legitimus*, meaning legal. But legitimacy is not limited to legality; it also relates to conscience and values. In this sense, legitimacy is a value judgment superimposed onto legality. We must therefore differentiate between formal legitimacy, based on the law, and social legitimacy, which is rooted in the symbolic norms shared by the members of a society. Initially, Weber's work, based on a highly normative measure of legitimacy seen as conformity to laws, evolved towards a more utilitarian perspective that took into account the interests of the public in evaluation criteria (Gabriel 2006). Suchman (1995, p. 574) is illustrative of this more utilitarian approach by integrating a pragmatic component to his conceptualization of legitimacy, which he defines as "a generalized perception or presumption that an entity's actions are desirable, proper, or appropriate within a socially constructed system of norms, values, beliefs, and definitions". By transposition, a patient's actions would be legitimate if they were desirable, suitable or appropriate.

Organizational legitimacy is the subject of a vast literature that, according to Suchman (1995), is structured around two main approaches: a strategic approach and an institutional one. The *strategic* approach (Dowling and Pfeffer 1975; Ashforth and Gibbs 1990; Zimmerman and Zeitz 2002) is based on a rather internal vision that views legitimacy as the product of an organization and as a resource that can be manipulated. From this perspective, this strategic approach is concerned with aspects of power and control over resources, as well as with forms of environmental influence (Reynaud and Walas 2015). It resonates with work on the resource-based view, which recognizes that organizations have both the power to acquire legitimacy by conforming to norms, and that they also have the capacity to intervene and modify these norms (Bitektine 2011). Organizational legitimacy is instrumentalized and perceived as a resource (Zimmerman and Zeitz 2002) by agents capable of "manipulating and deploying symbols" (Suchman 1995, p. 572) that will likely create the conditions for a convergence of perceptions. The ability of patients to change the healthcare system, such as achieving recognition of an illness, falls into this category. The *institutional* approach (Meyer and Rowan 1977; DiMaggio and Powell 1983; Suddaby 2010) takes an external view and focuses on aspects of conformity or isomorphism (Huault 2009). Legitimacy is granted by stakeholders and depends on the environment; it is an inevitable consequence of the socialization process. To a large extent, the health democracy at work fits into this second perspective.

Utilitarians reconcile these two approaches by conceiving legitimacy as both "a manipulable resource", as well as "a taken-for-granted belief system" (Suchman 1995, p. 577, cited in Reynaud and Walas 2015).

Legitimacy can be manipulated through substantive strategic processes, the implementation of actions or through communication (Ashforth and Gibbs 1990; Suchman 1995). Suchman presents a typology of strategies organized around the pragmatic, normative and cognitive dynamics available to the company to legitimize itself.

It is important to understand how an entity acquires legitimacy. Zimmerman and Zeitz (2002, p. 415) identify four legitimization strategies: conformation, selection, manipulation and creation, the characteristics of which are summarized in Table 7.1.

Conformation	Following the rules imposed by the social system, that is, acting "in accordance with the demands and expectations of the existing social structure" (Zimmerman and Zeitz 2002, p. 422). It may seem paradoxical for a new entity to seek legitimacy by conforming to existing norms. However, the conformation strategy can enhance a new entity's legitimacy by reinforcing the alignment of its actions with a social environment made up of established rules, norms and values.
Selection	Choosing, from among the set of rules, norms and values that make up its social environment, those with which it wishes to appear legitimate (Zimmerman and Zeitz 2002, p.423). It may be rational for a new entity to choose its scope of activities, its modes of action, and/or its geographical location with a view to selecting an environment conducive to its development.
Manipulation	The new entity must "change the environment" in order to guarantee coherence between itself and its environment (Zimmerman and Zeitz 2002, p. 424). For the new entity, this means controlling the social process of assessing its legitimacy by directly influencing it.
Creation	Introducing a normative, regulatory, technological and/or cultural breakthrough likely to transform the environment in which the new entity evolves. This is a form of "institutional entrepreneurship" (Zimmerman and Zeitz 2002, p. 425), fostering consonant perceptions of the new entity.

Table 7.1. *The four strategies of legitimization (adapted from Zimmerman and Zeitz (2002))*

In addition to this processual approach, other works have explored the different types of legitimacy. For example, Bitektine (2011) draws on a diversity of contexts to identify 18 types of legitimacy, which can be grouped around two forms: an active form involving deliberate examination of compliance with rules and norms, and a more passive, unconscious legitimacy assessment corresponding to the "taken-for-granted" nature of the object being evaluated (Alexiou and Wiggins 2019). The former refers to socio-political legitimacy, the latter to cognitive legitimacy (Aldrich and Fiol 1994; Bitektine 2011).

7.2.2.1. *Sociopolitical legitimacy*

Granting socio-political legitimacy "refers to the process by which key stakeholders, the general public, opinion leaders or government officials accept a company as appropriate and just, given existing norms and laws" (Aldrich and Fiol 1994, p. 648). The criteria for assessing sociopolitical legitimacy vary according to subject and context. Sociopolitical legitimacy has three dimensions. In its *regulatory dimension*, it refers to compliance with the legal and regulatory framework (Zimmerman and Zeitz 2002). In its pragmatic dimension, it the result that is looked at. It results from a "rational calculation" on the part of agents belonging to the organization's environment (Suchman 1995, p. 578). This dimension focuses on the public's own interests (Suchman 1995). It is based on the assessment of the value and benefits brought by the entity being evaluated to its stakeholders. Finally, the *moral or normative dimension* reflects "a positive normative evaluation of the organization and its activities" (Suchman 1995, p. 579). It is based on consequences (legitimacy of consequences), such as the pursuit of societal well-being, the procedures and techniques mobilized to act (procedural legitimacy), the ability to perform certain actions (structural legitimacy) and the individual qualities of the actors who embody it (personal legitimacy) (Suchman 1995, pp. 579–581).

7.2.2.2. *Cognitive legitimacy*

This second form of legitimacy is based on cognition (i.e. comprehensibility), rather than interest or evaluation. It refers to what is comprehensible and obvious, or "taken for granted" (Suchman 1995; Alexiou and Wiggins 2019). This type of legitimacy is also about familiarity: its passive character comes "from widely held beliefs and taken-for-granted assumptions" (Scott 1994, p. 81) that are based on socially constructed cultural elements, which in turn provide evaluators with a framework for measuring legitimacy (Scott 2010). This form is considered the most stable and enduring type of legitimacy (Suchman 1995; Scott 2008). In its strongest form, it reflects the public's tacit approval of an uncontested reality and dispenses with an active assessment of legitimacy.

Table 7.2 summarizes the key characteristics of the two main forms of legitimacy.

<table>
<tr><th colspan="2">Sociopolitical legitimacy</th></tr>
<tr><td>Regulatory legitimacy</td><td>– Emerging from compliance with the law or other forms of collective regulation
– Focuses on regulatory processes, rules and standards, and expectations created by governing bodies, trade associations and other influential organizations</td></tr>
<tr><td>Pragmatic legitimacy</td><td>– Acts on image and relationships to show consideration for the social system of stakeholders
– Takes into account the public's own interests
– Is based on an assessment of the value and benefits provided by the entity being evaluated to its stakeholders.
– Is judged by the results and consequences of the entity or its actions</td></tr>
<tr><td>Moral (or normative) legitimacy</td><td>– Concerns the correct ways of doing things and establishing leaders, practices, structures and processes that will be perceived positively by stakeholders</td></tr>
<tr><th colspan="2">Cognitive legitimacy</th></tr>
<tr><td>Cognitive legitimacy</td><td>– Aims to embed itself in the collective unconscious to be understood by stakeholders and become indispensable
– Refers to the comprehensible, evident, familiar or "taken for granted" nature that entities or practices acquire as they institutionalize</td></tr>
</table>

Table 7.2. *Dimensions of sociopolitical and cognitive legitimacy and their characteristics (adapted from Reynaux and Walas (2015) and Bouhaddane (2022))*

Based on a review of typologies, Deephouse et al. (2017) propose assessing legitimacy on the basis of cognitive, pragmatic, moral and regulatory criteria.

7.3. Methodology

In order to uncover the processes involved in building the legitimacy of patient action around long Covid, I conducted a case study (Kozinets 2010) of a long Covid patient association. I used all of the materials produced by the association from April 2020 to April 2022, and messages posted on X (Twitter) by *Association Covid Long France*'s account. I traced the events chronologically from April 2020, when patients launched the hashtag

#ApresJ20 on X (Twitter) to draw attention to the persistence of symptoms beyond the initial 15 to 20 days after a Covid-19 infection. I conducted a content analysis of the information available from messages posted on X and discussion forums, documents produced, interviews and testimonials.

It was the subject of the research, long Covid, a very recent and controversial phenomenon, which informed the choice of research methods. It was not possible to identify long Covid patients and interview them in order to understand the consequences of persistent symptoms on their health and their lives. The coding of patient followed the conventional procedure (Saldana 2011). It was built around the dimensions of experience (cognitive, emotional, social, sensory and behavioral (Hirschman and Holbrook 1982; Holbrook and Hirschman 1982; Lemon and Verhoef 2016)) to which I added the physical one, given the particularity of the subject treated (effect of a virus). The other data (messages posted on X, interviews, documents produced) were used to retrace the chronological evolution of the association's actions. In this way, we were able to highlight different periods of time by mobilizing the presented framework of legitimacy around the socio-political (pragmatic, moral, regulatory) and cognitive dimensions.

7.4. Results

7.4.1. *Getting to know oneself and being recognized: avoiding invisibility*

In April 2020, six people met on the Internet to share their experiences of the physical (fatigue, pain, etc.) and psychological (difficulty concentrating, depression, etc.) symptoms following a Covid-19 infection. In May 2020, they set up a collective to document their symptoms and publicize their health situation. In October 2020, the *Association Covid Long France* was born. In the words of the association's founders, its aim was to bring together the knowledge acquired through monitoring and gathering available information to inform and support affected patients:

> We have united as a collective to gather acquired knowledge (including monitoring press articles and international scientific research), create information media (such as posters and websites), contact journalists, MPs, doctors, politicians, to provide support for sufferers and to make our voices heard in

the hope of being recognized and cured one day. (Founders of the association)

Their ambition was to unite on and inform about long Covid in collaboration with researchers and doctors and to provide support for sufferers. Their four objectives were to achieve recognition of long Covid based on symptoms, not just tests; to communicate with doctors and the general public; to develop multidisciplinary care in all regions and to develop research involving patients.

We can identify different stages in the process of emergence and legitimization of what we can call long Covid (Covid with persistent symptoms) pathology.

7.4.2. *Stages in the legitimization process*

7.4.2.1. *Gathering experience as the basis of cognitive pragmatic legitimacy*

The first step was to develop a knowledge base to create a cognitive foundation, firstly for patients, so that they could see that the situation they were experiencing (altered state of health beyond 21 days following a Covid-19 infection) was not unique. Their experience, although very personal, was also experienced by other patients. During this phase, we documented the disease using numerous testimonials in which people described their symptoms, state of health and personal situation (i.e. the impact of these symptoms on their lives) in detail. The aim was to use real-life situations to provide a detailed description of what long Covid sufferers were experiencing. The aim was to bring about valid, constructed collective knowledge by building up a knowledge base: individual, local knowledge, anchored in the moment and confronted with the experience of others. This collective sharing helped to establish convergences regarding the manifestation of long Covid symptoms. People affected by these persistent symptoms expressed their dismay at the skepticism of those around them as well as medical professionals, which led to numerous treatment errors or a lack of treatment. The aim was to show that the situations experienced by the patients (despite clinical examinations that were potentially described as inconclusive) were not just a figment of the patients' imagination (somatic disorder), but that they were a very real quantitative phenomenon that deserved attention:

> My stomach hurts. Excruciating, unbearable pain… I am "burning" from the inside, I "feel" my food moving through my intestines… I'm inhabited by a beast!!!! I found myself out of breath going up the stairs on February 27 and I don't feel well at all… I can't even take a shower, I can't feel my legs, they're shaking. I can't bring myself to… I can't stay like this. I take a shower sitting down because standing is too much effort – I'm only 19! I asked my doctor about it, and they told me it's quite strange. (Émilie, 19 years old)

This essential step made it possible to document long Covid symptoms that had not yet been researched – the first scientific articles were only published a few months later in 2020 (Carfi et al. 2020; Harding 2020).

7.4.2.2. *Time for media coverage: making known and labeling*

This second stage involved the production of organized and structured information in order to contribute to the development of patient knowledge. The information targets were many: patients and their families, and parents of young children affected by the disease, to deconstruct representations (such as "children don't develop serious symptoms") and, ultimately, to educate. It also involves addressing employers who may have difficulty accepting and understanding their employees' sick leave. The discourse was legitimized by a strong scientific foundation, by citing and making accessible scientific papers published in major scientific journals and by academic societies (e.g. *The Lancet*). The aim of this stage was to enable patients and their relatives to put a "label" on their state of health and thus reduce the anxiety caused by being unable to describe and categorize it. Ultimately, it was about enabling patients to exist as sufferers of long Covid, to be identifiable and identified as such. The *ApresJ20* association helped to fill the gap in information resources. For both the association and the patients, this step also allowed the advocacy to be brought to the attention of institutions and members of parliament and to foster collaborations with international groups of long Covid patients, with a view to sharing experiences. At the same time, a worldwide network of long Covid patient associations was being set up, as the phenomenon was global.

7.4.2.3. *Moving up the political agenda*

In February 2021, the *ApresJ20* association was invited by the *Haute Autorité de santé* (French National Authority for Health) to help develop a rapid response to the management of patients suffering from the symptoms of long Covid, alongside other associations (such as *TousPartenairesCovid* and MillionsMissingFrance). The association was heard by the Minister of Health. During this time, numerous webinars and public relations initiatives took place in order to establish the long Covid issue in the media and the political sphere. This is the emergence of long Covid as a political issue, with the objective for the association of achieving its recognition as a (chronic) disease.

7.4.2.4. *The affirmation of scientificity and professionalization*

The *ApresJ20* association identified research themes linked to clinicians. It sought funding, it forged partnerships with researchers for the development of research programs and, at the same time, it trained expert patients within the framework of patient universities so that they could work with the Regional Health Agency tasked by the French Ministry of Health to consider the implementation of long Covid care pathways. An analysis of these times could help to identify the process of recognizing long Covid patient expertise.

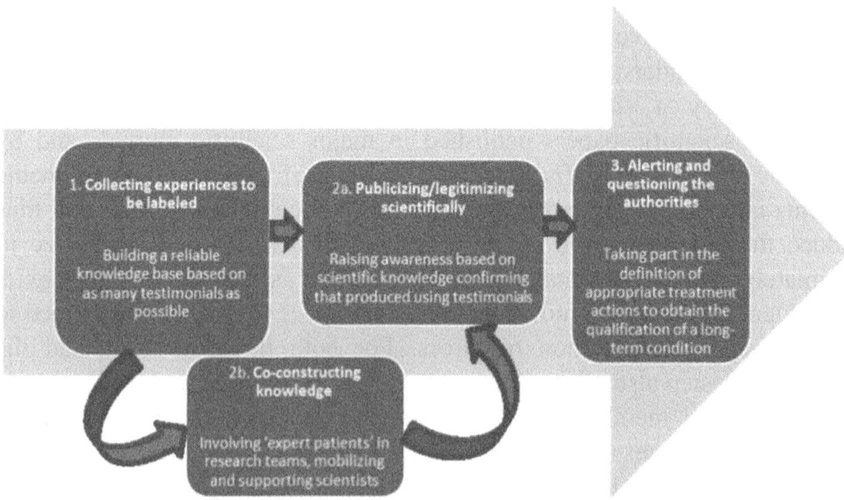

Figure 7.1. *Recognition process of long Covid patient expertise (source: Rochette (2023))*

7.5. Discussion

This case study highlights the need to draw on the expertise born of patient experience, particularly in situations where it is not appropriate to rely on standardization of clinical practices and the medical logic of evidence-based medicine, due to a lack of benchmarks and insufficiently documented clinical cases. In a context in which patients' contributions and lay knowledge are still all too often ignored, giving more space to patient expertise is a major challenge, one that requires the medical and nursing professions to assimilate the scope of lay knowledge.

This case study has revealed the simultaneous presence of four strategies of legitimization (Zimmerman and Zeitz 2002). Initially, the collective conforms to the rules imposed by the social system (conformation strategy) by adopting a scientific approach in order to demonstrate the existence of long Covid symptoms in the scientific sphere. The collective then clearly defines its scope of intervention: to raise awareness of the issue and to gain recognition, as well as to bring about effective care (selection strategy). The collective next seeks to mobilize the political sphere, which is more akin to a strategy of influence than manipulation, in order to influence regulatory texts (recognition of a long-term disease), and ultimately transform the environment (creation strategy). These strategies activate the different dimensions of legitimacy as identified by Suchman (1995).

One of *ApresJ20*'s first priorities was to obtain regulatory legitimacy by complying with standards (particularly scientific standards), based on good practice (moral legitimacy), so that the perception of the association's actions and the very existence of the association, as well as its activities, are the subject of a positive normative evaluation. The association's representatives clearly emphasized public interests (including public health, and the economic and social impact of long Covid) and their desire to contribute to the development of effective patient care. In so doing, they activated a pragmatic legitimacy: that these patients could have access to appropriate care. The collective was not content with just being a discussion group on social networks (*#ApresJ20*); it formed an association and developed increasingly organized practices. Patient volunteers were able to benefit from training at the Patients' University (Sorbonne University), so they could integrate working and research groups, with the right codes and ways of doing things. We could even speak of a certain professionalization. This established the group's moral legitimacy, insofar as the members and practices were perceived positively by the stakeholders. The group/collective also worked to acquire regulatory legitimacy by drawing on foreign examples and legal texts and by questioning decision-makers. Cognitive legitimacy was probably trickier to establish, since the persistent symptoms following Covid-19 infection were not always known or understood by professionals. The symptoms were not evident or "self-evident," especially as the virus mutated, giving rise to new variants and diverse manifestations of infection, which were also generally attenuated by vaccination.

The symptoms of long Covid are also characteristic of other health situations and/or pathologies. As medical and epidemiological research has shown, it is not always easy to link persistent symptoms to a Covid-19 infection, yet this is where the added value of a patient experience comes in. This work has enabled us to cross-reference the strategies of legitimization with the dimensions of legitimacy.

As we can see, the work of long Covid patients has accelerated the process of general recognition of the disease by creating a dynamic of knowledge accumulation, on the one hand, to emerge from anonymity and, on the other hand, to speed up the agenda for "faster" action on health policy. This case highlights how digital media, including social media networks have catalyzed this process: long Covid has since become a recognizable "scientific subject" (Daston 2000) and has also been taken up by the WHO.

7.6. Conclusion

This research sheds light on the value of patient experience, particularly in the case of new health situations, and responds to the need for more detailed knowledge of patient experience using qualitative methods of analysis (Clavel et al. 2019). This research, which began as an attempt to understand the experience of persistent symptoms for French Covid-19 patients, reveals how patient experience could be legitimized, leading to recognition of the expertise developed by the patient collective.

The updated legitimation process also highlights the activation of three of the four dimensions of legitimacy studied. Cognitive legitimacy requires, on the one hand, an institutionalization of entities and, on the other hand, a collective incorporation of the manifestations of long Covid, so that they are considered "self-evident". However, the mutations of the virus, with the potentially attenuated effects of the new variants and its possible eventual disappearance, make the case of long Covid unique. Indeed, it takes time to both build expertise and gain recognition. Given the highly changeable nature of Covid-19, this expertise may not have enough time to establish itself and thus acquire the scientific legitimacy that other patient associations have been able to acquire. We can underline the important role of patient experience.

7.7. References

Aldrich, H.E. and Fiol, C.M. (1994). Fools rush in? The institutional context of industry creation. *Academy of Management Review*, 19(4), 645–670.

Alexiou, K. and Wiggins, J. (2019). Measuring individual legitimacy perceptions: Scale development and validation. *Strategic Organization*, 17(4), 470–496.

Anderson, R.M. and Funnell, M.M. (2010). Patient empowerment: Myths and misconceptions. *Patient Education and Counseling*, 79(3), 277–282.

Ashforth, B.E. and Gibbs, B.W. (1990). The double-edge of organizational legitimation. *Organization Science*, 1(2), 177–194.

Berkman, N.D., Davis, T.C., McCormack, L. (2010). Health literacy: What is it? *Journal of Health Communication*, 15(S2), 9–19.

Bitektine, A. (2011). Toward a theory of social judgments of organizations: The case of legitimacy, reputation, and status. *Academy of Management Review*, 36(1), 151–179.

Boudier, F., Oudier, F., Bensebaa, F., Jablanczy, A. (2012). L'émergence du patient-expert : une perturbation innovante. *Innovations*, 3, 13–25.

Bouhaddane, M. (2022). La légitimité perçue des labels alimentaires : quel impact sur la confiance des consommateurs et sur la valeur perçue des produits alimentaires labellisés? PhD Thesis, Université Clermont Auvergne, Clermont-Ferrand.

Broeckaert, L. and Challacombe, L. (2014). Health navigation: A review of the evidence. *CATIE: Prevention in Focus* [Online]. Available at: http://www.catie.ca/en/pif/fall-2014/health-navigationreview-evidence.

Callard, F. and Perego, E. (2021). How and why patients made Long Covid. *Social Science & Medicine*, 268(113426), 1–5.

Carfì, A., Bernabei, R., and Landi, F.; for the Gemelli Against COVID-19 Post-Acute Care Study Group (2020). Persistent symptoms in patients after acute COVID-19. *JAMA*, 324(6), 603–605.

Castro, E.M., Van Regenmortel, T., Vanhaecht, K., Sermeus, W., Van Hecke, A. (2016). Patient empowerment, patient participation and patient-centeredness in hospital care: A concept analysis based on a literature review. *Patient Education and Counseling*, 99(12), 1923–1939.

Clavel, N., Pomey, M.P., Ghadiri, D.P.S. (2019). Partnering with patients in quality improvement: Towards renewed practices for healthcare organization managers? *BMC Health Services Research*, 19(1), 1–12.

Cotterrell, R. (1997). *Legality and Legitimacy: The Sociology of Max Weber. Law's Community: Legal Theory in Sociological Perspective*. Oxford University Press, Oxford.

Dahl Rendtorff, J. (2021). Principes éthiques communs et biopolitique à l'époque du covid-19. *Diogène*, 3, 37–49.

Daston, L. (ed.) (2000). Introduction: The coming into being of scientific objects. In *Biographies of Scientific Objects*. The University of Chicago Press, Chicago.

Deephouse, D.L. and Suchman, M. (2008). Legitimacy in organizational institutionalism. In *The Sage Handbook of Organizational Institutionalism*, Greenwood, R., Oliver, C., Sahlin, K., Suddaby, R. (eds). Sage, London.

Deephouse, D.L., Bundy, J., Tost, L.P., and Suchman, M.C. (2017). Organizational legitimacy: Six key questions. In *The SAGE Handbook of Organizational Institutionalism*, Greenwood, R., Oliver, C., Lawrence, T., Meyer, R. (eds). Sage, London.

Dewey, J. (2004). *Comment nous pensons*. Editions Les Empêcheurs de penser en rond, Paris.

Dimaggio, P.J. and Powell, W.W. (1983). The iron cage revisited: Institutional isomorphism and collective rationality in organizational fields. *American Sociological Review*, 147–160.

Dowling, J. and Pfeffer, J. (1975). Organizational legitimacy: Social values and organizational behavior. *Pacific Sociological Review*, 18(1), 122–136.

Duvall, C.K. (1999). Developing individual freedom to act: Empowerment in the knowledge organization. *Participation and Empowerment: An International Journal*, 7(8), 204–212.

Flora, L. (2013). Le patient formateur dans le système de santé : méthodologie de recherche dans le cadre d'une thèse en sciences de l'éducation. *Recherches qualitatives*, 15, 166–185.

Freeman, H.P. (2012). The origin, evolution, and principles of patient navigation. *Cancer Epidemiology, Biomarkers & Prevention*, 21(10), 1614–1617.

Freeman, H.P. and Rodriguez, R.L. (2011). History and principles of patient navigation. *Cancer*, 117(S15), 3537–3540.

Gabriel, P. (2006). Le système de légitimité de l'entreprise responsable : délimitations et dynamique. *AIMS, Actes de la XVe Conférence Internationale de Management Stratégique*, June, 1–28 [Online]. Available at: https://www.strategie-aims.com/conferences/8-xveme-conference-de-l-aims/communications/2269-le-systeme-de-legitimite-de-lentreprise-responsable-delimitations-et-dynamique/download.

Harding, L. (2020). "Weird as hell": The Covid-19 patients who have symptoms for months. *The Guardian* [Online]. Available at: https://www.theguardian.com/world/2020/may/15/weird-hell-professor-advent-calendar-covid-19-symptoms-paul-garner.

Holbrook, M.B. and Hirschman, E.C. (1982a). The experiential aspects of consumption: Consumer fantasies, feelings, and fun. *Journal of Consumer Research*, 9(2), 132–140.

Holbrook, M.B. and Hirschman, E.C. (1982b). Hedonic consumption: Emerging concepts, methods and propositions. *Journal of Marketing*, 46(3), 92–101.

Holmström, I. and Röing, M. (2010). The relation between patient-centeredness and patient empowerment: A discussion on concepts. *Patient Education and Counseling*, 79(2), 167–172.

Huault, I. (2009). *Paul DiMaggio et Walter W. Powell - des organisations en quête de légitimité*. Éditions EMS, Caen.

Kauffmann, I. (2014). Les trois types purs de la domination légitime de Max Weber : les paradoxes de la domination et de la liberté. *Sociologie*, 5(3), 307–317.

Kickbusch, I., Pelikan, J.M., Apfel, F., Tsouros, A.D. (2013). *Health Literacy: The Solid Facts*. WHO Regional Office for Europe, Copenhagen.

Klein, A. (2014). Au-delà du masque de l'expert. Réflexions sur les ambitions, enjeux et limites de l'Éducation Thérapeutique du Patient. Report, Rééducation orthophonique.

Košir, U. and Sørensen, K. (2022). COVID-19: The key to flattening the curve is health literacy. *Perspectives in Public Health*, 142(5), 259–260.

Kozinets, R.V. (2006). Netnography. In *Handbook of Qualitative Research Methods in Marketing*, Belk, R.W. (ed.). Edward Elgar Publishing, Cheltenham.

Lemon, K.N. and Verhoef, P.C. (2016). Understanding customer experience throughout the customer journey. *Journal of Marketing*, 80(6), 69–96.

Meyer, J.W. and Rowan, B. (1977). Institutionalized organizations: Formal structure as myth and ceremony. *American Journal of Sociology*, 83(2), 340–363.

Nutbeam, D. (1999). Literacies across the lifespan: Health literacy. *Literacy and Numeracy Studies*, 9(2), 47–55.

Nutbeam, D. (2008). The evolving concept of health literacy. *Social Science & Medicine*, 67(12), 2072–2078.

Osborne, M. (ed.) (2012). *Health Literacy from A to Z*. Jones & Bartlett Publishers, Burlington.

Osborne, R.R., Batterham, R.W., Elsworth, G.R., Hawkins, M., Buchbinder, R. (2013). The grounded psychometric development and initial validation of the Health Literacy Questionnaire (HLQ). *BMC Public Health*, 13(1), 1–17.

Perego, E., Callard, F., Stras, L., Melville-Jóhannesson, B., Pope, R., Alwan, N.A. (2020). Why the patient-made term "long Covid" is needed. *Wellcome Open Research*, 5(224), 224.

Pomey, M.-P., Flora, L., Karazivan, P., Dumez, V., Lebel, P., Vanier, M.-C., Débarges, B., Clavel, N., Jouet, E. (2015). Le "Montreal model" : enjeux du partenariat relationnel entre patients et professionnels de la santé. *Santé publique*, 1, 41–50.

Rabeharisoa, V. and Callon, M. (2002). L'engagement des associations de malades dans la recherche. *Revue internationale des sciences sociales*, 1, 65–73.

Rappaport, J. (1987). Terms of empowerment/exemplars of prevention: Toward a theory for community psychology. *American Journal of Community Psychology*, 15(2), 121.

Reynaud, E. and Walas, A. (2015). Discours sur la RSE dans le processus de légitimation de la banque. *Revue française de gestion*, 41(248), 187–209.

Saldaña, J. (2011). *Fundamentals of Qualitative Research*. Oxford University Press, Oxford.

Scott, W.R. (1994). Conceptualizing organizational fields: Linking organizations and societal systems. *Systemrationalitat und partialinteresse*, 203–221.

Scott, W.R. (2008). Approaching adulthood: The maturing of institutional theory. *Theory and Society*, 37, 427–442.

Scott, W.R. (2010). Entrepreneurs and professionals: The mediating role of institutions. In *Institutions and Entrepreneurship*, Sine, W.D. and David, R.J. (eds). Emerald Group Publishing Limited, Bingley.

Sørensen, K., Van den Broucke, S., Fullam, J., Doyle, G., Pelikan, J., Slonska, Z., Brand, H. (2012). Health literacy and public health: A systematic review and integration of definitions and models. *BMC Public Health*, 12(1), 1–13.

Staples, L.H. (1990). Powerful ideas about empowerment. *Administration in Social Work*, 14(2), 29–42.

Suchman, M.C. (1995). Managing legitimacy: Strategic and institutional approaches. *Academy of Management Review*, 20(3), 571–610.

Suddaby, R. (2010). Challenges for institutional theory. *Journal of Management Inquiry*, 19(1), 14–20.

Wolf, J.A., Niederhauser, V., Marshburn, D., LaVela, S.L. (2014). Defining patient experience. *Patient Experience Journal*, 1(1), 7–19.

Yong, E. (2020). Long-haulers are redefining COVID-19. *The Atlantic* [Online]. Available at: https://www.theatlantic.com/health/archive/2020/06/covid-19-coronavirus-longterm-symptoms-months/612679/.

Zimmerman, M.A. and Zeitz, G.J. (2002). Beyond survival: Achieving new venture growth by building legitimacy. *Academy of Management Review*, 27(3), 414–431.

8

Patient Influencers: Towards a Double Layer of Expertise

8.1. Introduction

Lay expertise in healthcare has been the subject of a growing body of research in recent decades (see, for example, Grimaldi (2010); Akrich and Rabeharisoa (2012)). Recent work in information and communication sciences (Djahanchahi et al. 2021) has demonstrated that patient expertise takes many forms and can be valorized in a variety of ways (see Table 8.1).

With the rise of social media and the influencer, patients can easily share their experiential expertise via their own means and, in doing so, create a community around them. Patient influencers can be positioned as "ordinary prescribers" to their own "sociodigital network" (Stenger 2011, p. 132). In this chapter, we will look at the mobilization of experiential health knowledge by patients who have become influencers on social networks and at the instrumentalization of influencers, particularly as part of influencer marketing strategies.

8.2. Literature review and research questions

Charmaz's (2000) work on the experience of chronic illness has demonstrated that patients become veritable experts in their health condition, akin to healthcare professionals, since they have to live with and manage it on a daily basis. The notion of healthcare expertise is vast and covers a diverse

Chapter written by Oihana HUSSON.

array of actors. As Djahanchahi et al. (2021, p. 180) point out, "expertise refers to an individual's ability to offer a diagnosis that is informed by legitimate knowledge in a given situation". The different types of expertise that can be found in the healthcare sector are presented in Table 8.1.

Type of expertise	Recognition mode	Space for expression	Main legitimization
Academic	Degrees, a career compartmentalized into the fields in which the subject trained	Agencies, media, reports, conferences, profession and public debate	Medical institutional
Technical-professional	Career ladder, professional experience	Professional environment, agencies, reports, media and public debate	Medical institutional
Experiential	Recounting experiences (professional or from everyday life) which constitutes a structure recognized by peers	Professional environment, communities of interest or practice, life stories and media	Institutional, associative or community
Lay	Subject's professional experience, outside of a career or academic recognition	Medical circles, communities of interest or practice, forums and blogs	Community first, then medical institutional
Warm (non-professionals who help less experienced individuals)	At close quarters, able to explain technical terms, to popularize	Discussion forums, workshops, fab labs and communities of interest or practice	Community
Citizen	Linked to unions and the struggles and demands of a movement. These experts speak out against practices that are legal but which they consider unacceptable	Citizen protests, public meetings and public debate	Associative institutional
Collective	Similar to citizen expertise. Depends on the number of actors who speak on the same subject	Discussion forums, workshops, fab labs, communities of interest or practice and public debate	Associative institutional
Community	Claimed by communities of practice, interest or epistemology. Implies compartmentalization from the rest of society	Discussion forums, workshops, fab labs and communities of interest or practice	Community

Table 8.1. *Types of expertise, origins, areas of expression and main modes of legitimization (source: Djahanchahi et al. (2021, p. 194))*

Academic expertise and technical–professional expertise are the most widely recognized forms of expertise in society, particularly given the role they play in public decision-making. They derive from institutionalized knowledge, which in turn gives them a sacred character; the information provided by academic and professional experts has long been considered incontestable. Conversely, lay expertise sits in opposition to this "institutional transcendence" (Djahanchahi et al. 2021, p. 193). For Grimaldi (2010), lay expertise is the product of three societal facts: the critique of scientific expertise, the existence of experiential knowledge and the dissemination of knowledge, particularly by new communication technologies. In this way, lay experts can share their expertise with other patients in whatever format they choose. By sharing their experience online, lay experts can become a resource for "new patients" (Bolam et al. 2003) seeking out information and social support (Cherba et al. 2019).

When peer support workers volunteer their services, their lay expertise is considered indisputable. However, their professional integration poses problems, not least because it is difficult to define what constitutes the peer support work. In addition, professionalization raises the question of training and access to it: What training for what role(s)? (Delaquaize et al. 2021). We should also note that a patient who is a resource for others does not need to be a model patient and is under no obligation to train and take courses in medicine or communication (Grimaldi 2010). In short, they need no validation from the medical profession to share their experiences with others.

The emergence of social media and the influencer's role raises the question of how to monetize patient-generated content. Here, we will focus on patients who use social media to share their healthcare experiences. They become "infomediaries": mediators and resources (Frau-Meigs 2017) for a condition and its management. The question is that of the twofold professionalization of the patient, both as a peer helper and influencer.

8.3. Methodology

This study will draw on research carried out as part of my doctoral thesis in information and communication sciences, in order to analyze the phenomenon of patients becoming social media influencers. I will use four Instagram accounts of patients with congenital melanocytic nevus (giant CMN), selected via a monitoring process, as the basis for this study.

Giant CMN is a dermatological pathology characterized by the presence of large dermatological lesions from birth – comparable to giant moles due to pigmentation – and the presence of uneven bumpy surfaces and hairs. This pathology results in a mark in Goffman's (1975) sense and raises the question of online self-presentation. I categorized the posts of the selected Instagram accounts and conducted a diachronic analysis, which enabled me to highlight a process of professionalization of influence on social media. I analyzed a total of 670 posts from February 2013 to July 2021.

This analysis was complemented by three semi-structured interviews with three representatives of advertising agencies that provide influencer marketing services. Two of the agencies were located in France (Professionals no. 1 and 3), while the third was located in Canada and also managed campaigns in America (Professional no. 2). Conducting semi-structured interviews allowed for flexibility and for a comparative analysis of the data. The interview guides covered the course of the marketing campaigns and the specificities of the healthcare sector.

Finally, I examined the Instagram communications of brands founded by Yulianna Yussef, a healthcare influencer whose account I studied in my initial analysis, Neviscope and Nevicosmetics.

I carried out an analysis of the posts on the brands' Instagram accounts, focusing on iconographic and textual data, in order to analyze the use of storytelling and the experience of the brands' founder.

8.4. Discussion of results

8.4.1. *The importance of legitimacy*

Throughout the interviews with influencer marketing professionals, they continually emphasized the importance of working with influencers who have a legitimate voice. This legitimacy was acquired through expertise in a specific field. The professionals we met expressed the importance of an influencer's expert status:

> For me, [an influencer], is first and foremost an opinion leader who has specialized in a subject and, over time, acquired visibility and credibility, without any outside help. [...] If they're followed for their expertise, they will likely be a good

> fit for clients. (Professional no. 1, interviewed December 8, 2021)

> That's what makes it legitimate for an influencer to speak out. If, tomorrow, I have a lifestyle influencer who talks to me about car repairs or bodywork, he won't be legitimate. I'm not interested. (Professional no. 3, interviewed on March 17, 2022)

We are living in an era in which many actors are speaking out on health issues, including a growing number of expert figures online (Vigouroux-Zugasti 2018). It is in the interest of the various speakers to implement strategies to capture the attention of Internet users and to establish their legitimacy, which is synonymous with validity (Eraly 2017). Among them, patients-come-influencers stand out by highlighting their personal experience and feelings, as well as adopting a vocabulary that popularizes medical terms.

8.4.2. *Building influence: from lay expertise to peer support*

A diachronic study of CMN patient accounts has revealed a process of professionalization over time (Husson and Sedda 2022). While they started as casual users, they acquired influencer status by creating a community around themselves and their content. Table 8.2 summarizes the accounts covered by our analysis and their various characteristics.

In this study, I was particularly interested in exposing the disease's stigma to the public eye. For some patients, depending on the location of the nevus and nevi clusters, the visibility (or rather, invisibility) of their condition is not a choice. Nevertheless, we may note that this visibility could be conscious and instrumentalized, in a search for recognition on a political level (Ancet 2018). Sometimes, the highlighting of scars was achieved through adherence to dominant aesthetic norms (Husson and Sedda 2022). This was particularly the case with the accounts of @robiarcuri and @yulianna.yussef, who post professional-quality snapshots that meet the societal beauty norms, such as slimness or trendy outfits[1].

1 See for example this photograph from Yussef's Instagram account (@yulianna.yussef), from January 21, 2021: https://www.instagram.com/p/CKTnPOrJiLz/?igsh=cGtwYTY4bHFwY3R0&img_index=1.

Account name	Number of followers	Number of posts studied	Comments
@yulianna.yussef	117 K	253	Model
@luna.love.hope	370 K	150	Baby account run by parents
@robiarcuri	8,831	47	Dancer
@lovingmydots	15.8 K	220	Speaker

Table 8.2. *Summary of the study conducted by Husson and Sedda (2022)*

If the mark was visible in a large number of posts, experiential expertise held a variable place in the editorial line of each Instagram account. On @yulianna.yussef's and @loving-mydots' Instagram accounts, the aim was to promote a motivational discourse focused on resilience. Conversely, on @luna.love.hope's account, the majority of the content was focused on care pathways.

The number of followers of the accounts studied varied in size. Using the follower count, I was able to classify them into different categories of influencer: macro-influencer (100,000 followers or more), nano-influencer (for smaller followings) and micro-influencer (between 30,000 and 100,000 followers).[2] These metrics and classifications are used in particular in influencer marketing to select the influencers with whom they wish to collaborate.

By investigating how the messages promoted by influencers with CMN are received by their peers (Husson and Sedda 2022), I was able to observe various benefits, in terms of motivation, awareness and normalization, through the visibility of the pathology, and finally, the questioning of aesthetic norms within society. It should be pointed out, however, that the influencer figure is the subject of criticism within the peer community, which points to the dissonance of creating a personal brand through the display of scarcity. The figure of the health influencer reveals the conflicts at work in capitalist society: while the sharing of experience is a matter of peer-help, the body is nonetheless exposed, put into figures and reinforces society's aesthetic and gendered norms.

2 See: https://www.journalducm.com/; https://www.journalducm.com/4-types-influenceurs-pour-vos-cam pagnes/.

8.4.3. *The professionalization of influencers as content creators*

This study of CMN patient Instagram accounts highlighted a process of professionalization. Indeed, the diachronic study reveals this transition from personal to professional use: over time, we can see a more regular upload schedule, an improvement in the quality of photography and a more defined editorial line.

The professionals we interviewed emphasized that being an influencer is a profession in its own right. It not only involves producing social media content, but also working to unite a community:

> Today, it's a job. Clearly. It's a new job. We see lots of people making a living from it, and it's very new. Five years ago, it wasn't a job. Today, it's a real job. (Professional no. 3, interviewed December 14, 2021)

> When there's regular work going into it, followers are receptive. You're going to have a lot of recurrence and a lot of credibility within that community. (Professional no. 1, interviewed December 8, 2021)

For influencers, it is imperative that they present themselves as credible experts on the topics they cover. This credibility is essential to expertise, which also refers to the notion of authority (Djahanchahi et al. 2021). In turn, this authority makes it possible for influencers to play a prescriptive role within the community. This attracts the attention of advertisers, who are eager to profit from the power of influence.

8.4.4. *Features specific to the healthcare sector*

The interviews with influencer marketing professionals also highlighted features specific to the healthcare sector. Firstly, there is an increased risk of controversy, which makes advertisers reluctant to use influencer marketing since their primary concern is to protect the company's image:

> No. It's a complicated area. It's hard to communicate on it. We don't have any clients in healthcare. (Professional no. 3, interviewed March 17, 2022)

> Few people attempt these kinds of campaigns, because it becomes complicated for everyone. (Professional no. 1, interviewed December 8, 2021)

While advertisers are reluctant to implement communication campaigns about healthcare products, advertising agencies are also cautious about protecting their image and seek to avoid controversy at all costs concerning the products or practices in question:

> We try to be careful about our image and whether we're consistent with what we're trying to do. Within the agency, there are projects that interest us much more than others. But it helps to protect the agency's image in the long term, that's clear. […] Each agency views its interests differently, depending on its business. For us, we're trying to find clients to sign on a regular basis, so we have to be careful about our image. It won't help if we end up in the press. (Professional no. 1, interviewed December 8, 2021)

> If we're doing prevention on health issues, why not? But when it comes to collaborating with a laboratory/pharmaceutical company, for one drug or another, I think it's more complicated. I worry about the reception. (Professional no. 3, interviewed March 17, 2022)

In addition, this risk also makes a number of influencers reluctant to dedicate most of their content to health-related topics:

> For the influencer, even if you come in offering a large sum of money, promising them 10,000 euros, if it's a sensitive subject, they're capable of saying no. You have to be able to convince them, to put forward the right arguments. Indeed, I think that's why we see very few operations set up on subjects like healthcare, especially complicated ones. (Professional no. 1, interviewed December 8, 2021)

In order to minimize the risk of controversy, health expertise is a necessity: "For me, the influencer has to be an expert to talk about health, and even more so in another field". (Professional no. 3, interviewed March 17, 2022)

Nevertheless, even though influencers can enjoy credibility within their community, the most coherent strategy is to unite the community around their person and the content they post at the service of other projects. By shifting their focus to other topics, influencers are not only able to grow their community, but this also helps to shield them from controversy.

The final special feature unique to the healthcare sector lies in its regulations:

> When collaborations take place, particularly with clients from sectors subject to regulations, as is the case with healthcare, the legal department is almost always involved to ensure that everything is in order. (Professional no. 2, interviewed December 14, 2021)

8.4.5. *Instrumentalization of influence in the service of other professional projects*

Through collaborations with brands, influencers have the opportunity to generate (variable) income, depending on the size of their community. In addition, they can also put their influence to good use on other professional projects. This is notably the case for Yussef, who has put her popularity to good use in a variety of professional projects, including modeling and the creation of two businesses.

While CMN is a source of stigma (Goffman 1975), it enables influencers to differentiate themselves and cultivate their personal brand (Amato 2016). In the case of Yussef, we see the use of personal branding through the creation of two brands: Neviscope and Nevicosmetics, both of which use the prefix "nevi," in reference to CMN. Neviscope is aimed at patients whose pathology requires increased monitoring of their skin and, more specifically, of nevi. It sells a dermatoscope that enables skin lesions to be photographed and sent to healthcare professionals, to reinforce the need to monitor and minimize risks. Nevicosmetics is aimed more at the general public and sells a sun cream. For both brands, Instagram provides the main channel for advertising.

Both the @nevicosmetics and @neviscope Instagram accounts focus on the founder's personality and experiences, given her lived experience with the disease[3].

The use of storytelling reinforces the expert's ethos, as Yussef draws on her experience as a patient. In addition, the description of Yussef evokes a certain resilience, as she presents herself as a patient who has turned her experience into strength and has achieved professional success as a result. Thus, in the context of peer-help, she promotes an image corresponding to the requirements for resilience and personal development.

In addition to sharing Yussef's personal experience, there are a large number of posts on Neviscope's and Nevicosmetic's Instagram accounts that share condensed medical information, particularly on dermatology[4].

The promotion of this knowledge, which is more akin to academic expertise, enables the brands to cultivate a serious image. At the same time, it allows Yussef to position herself once again as an expert, the editorial line of her Instagram account being partly centered around her role as business leader.

8.5. Conclusion

Recognition of patients' experiential knowledge has been fostered by progressive cooperation between patients and healthcare professionals, in line with the recommendations of the World Health Organization (WHO) and, in France, the law of January 2, 2002 (Liégeois and Didier 2021). In 2020, the *Comité éthique et cancer* (Ethics and Cancer Committee) in France issued a statement in favor of providing remuneration to expert patients[5]. Nevertheless, the *Fédération nationale de l'information médicale*[6] pointed

3 See for example this post from the @nevicosmetics2 account, uploaded November 10, 2021: https://www.instagram.com/p/CWFzwRlIUZv/?igsh=d3JjdnI1NzJ5eXFw.

4 See for example this post from the @neviscope account, uploaded January 8, 2020: https://www.instagram.com/p/B7EAoGJJ822/?igsh=MjI1amV1ejF0Z2tk.

5 Avis no. 36 – Éthique et cancer [Online]. Available at: https://www.ethique-cancer.fr/avis/avis-ndeg36 [Accessed October 25, 2022].

6 Fédération nationale de l'information médicale. Le "patient expert" : de qui et de quoi parle-t-on? [Online]. Available at: https://www.lafnim.com/actualite/le-patient-expert-de-qui-et-de-quoi-parle-t-on/164.htm [Accessed October 25, 2022].

out that members of parliament have opposed remuneration for time spent by a patient with their peers since 2009. What is more, in the majority of cases, the compensation system prohibits the remuneration of expert patients. As such, it appears to be easier for patients to make the most of their expertise outside of the healthcare sector than within it.

The professionalization of the influencer offers patients an opportunity to benefit financially from their experiential expertise outside the healthcare sector. The case of patient influencers raises the question of media coverage and recognition of lay expertise outside the healthcare system.

The question of opinion on profit generation is not anecdotal: it allows us to question the different representations regarding the monetization of expertise, when it is neither scientific nor formally recognized by an institution. The generation of profits from content posted by patients on social media can then be perceived as an emancipation from the medical profession, whose authority is called into question concerning the peer helper function. We see this as a twofold desecration of healthcare expertise: not only is the valued expertise not that of the medical profession, be it academic or technical-professional, but it can also be the subject of remuneration, notably through instrumentalization.

8.6. References

Amato, S. (2016). Développement de marque personnelle en ligne et influence sociale. *Communication et Organisation*, 65, 203–214.

Bolam, B., Gleeson, K., Murphy, S. (2003). Lay person or health expert? Exploring theoretical and practical. *Forum Qualitative Social Research. Aspects of Reflexivity in Qualitative Health Research*, 4(2), 26.

Cardon, D. (2019). *Culture numérique*. Presses de Sciences Po, Paris.

Cherba, M., Thoër C., Turbide O., Denault V., Renaud L., Valderrama A., Courcy I., Cordelier B., Laquerre M-E., Cyr C. et al. (2019). Le soutien social en ligne comme mode d'intervention psychosociale : revue de littérature, pistes de recherche et recommandations pour les intervenants. *Santé publique*, 31(1), 83–92. doi: 10.3917/spub.191.008.

Djahanchahi, S., Galibert, O., Cordelier, B. (2021). Towards an info-communication categorization of expertise in online health communities. In *Digital Health Communications*, Cordelier, B. and Galibert, O. (eds). ISTE Ltd, London, and John Wiley & Sons, New York.

Eraly, A. (2015). *Autorité et légitimité*. ERES, Toulouse.

Frau-Meigs, D. (2017). Les youtubeurs : les nouveaux influenceurs ! *Nectart*, 5(2), 126–136.

Galibert, O. (2021). La figure de l'érudit au risque d'Internet. *Hermès, La Revue*, 87(1), 181–188.

Goffman, E. (1975). *Stigmate. Les usages sociaux des handicaps.* Éditions de Minuit, Paris.

Honneth, A. (2020). *La reconnaissance : histoire européenne d'une idée.* Gallimard, Paris.

Husson, O. and Sedda, P. (2022). Quand la différence fait l'influence : stratégies et réception de l'exposition des corps atypiques sur Instagram. *Études de communication*, 58(1), 25–48.

Jost, F. (2013). *Le culte du banal. De Duchamp à la télé-réalité*. CNRS, Paris.

Massé, R. (2012). Expertises éthiques savantes et profanes en santé publique : défis et enjeux pour une éthique de la discussion. *Santé publique*, 24(1), 49–61.

Romeyer, H. (2021). The expert patient in the digital age: Between myth and reality. In *Digital Health Communications*, Cordelier, B. and Galibert, O. (eds). ISTE Ltd, London, and John Wiley & Sons, New York.

Stenger, T. (2011). La prescription de l'action collective. Double stratégie d'exploitation de la participation sur les réseaux socionumériques. *Hermès, La Revue*, 1(59), 127–133 [Online]. Available at: https://www-cairn-info.proxy-scd.u-bourgogne.fr/revue-hermes-la-revue-2011-1-page-127.htm.

Vigouroux-Zugasti, E. (2018). Experts et dispensateurs de conseils de santé en ligne : (en)jeux d'attention et de crédibilité. *Communication & Organisation*, 53(1), 145–158.

9

Legitimizing Lay Expertise: The Contribution of Terminology

9.1. Introduction

Terminology, as a discipline concerned with specialized discourse, is closely linked to the notions of *specialization* and *expertise*. Societal, technological and institutional changes in recent decades have led to significant changes that challenge the place of the expert and their knowledge in comparison to that of the general public who, from the absolute novice waiting to receive knowledge from the tutelary figure of the specialist, now has the minimum means to obtain information or even to develop *lay expertise*.

We can observe the breakdown of this specialist/non-specialist dichotomy in the medical field, in which the emergence of a participatory model (based on patient involvement in care and treatment) has caused the boundaries of expertise to fluctuate. This unprecedented situation in healthcare systems raises a number of questions, particularly with regards to terms and how they are used by actors in the field. From a terminology perspective, the question of links between terms and expertise is particularly interesting. This emerging context also poses a particular challenge to the notions of *appropriation* and *circulation of terms* between the different groups of actors in diabetology and the ways in which they participate in the recognition of forms of expertise. More generally, beyond the field of terminology, providing answers to these issues can help us to better

Chapter written by Emma THIBERT, Aurélie PICTON and Valérie DELAVIGNE.

understand these emerging forms of knowledge and to develop ways to assess their legitimacy.

In this chapter, we will present our preliminary observations and our preliminary results, as part of our ongoing research. By examining this changing medical context, specifically diabetology, and presenting the terminological issues at stake, we will show how a linguistic contribution fits into the debate on expertise and its legitimacy. We will outline our methodology, which includes a description of our data, the specificity of which is to present a hybridization between written productions and data from real-life situations. In order to concretize the possible contributions of terminology for evaluating the legitimacy of expertise, we propose three analyses inspired by methods in textual terminology and socioterminology.

9.2. Contextualization

The context and analyses we propose here constitute both a theoretical and methodological proposition made possible by the establishment of a new field of study. An overview of the discipline in which we are working, and of the framework in which we place our work, is therefore necessary before we turn to the methodology that will enable us to examine what we will call, at least provisionally in this chapter, the "linguistic legitimacy" of lay expertise.

9.2.1. *Terminology*

Terminology studies specialized discourse, defined by Moirand and Tréguer-Felten as "discourses constrained by an enunciation situation, which can be related to a professional social place (such as an institution, company, store, etc.), and which involve the transmission or exchange of theoretical or practical, declarative or procedural, or even experiential, information or knowledge between enunciators or interactants who have a defined socio-professional status or social position, and whose message has a precise pragmatic aim" (Moirand and Tréguer-Felten 2007, p. 5).

In our approach, the entry point for analysis is the term, understood as a lexical unit whose meaning is understood within a given discourse community. These terms provide evidence of the speakers' knowledge and can serve as markers of their expertise, provided that this usage is adapted to the medium (Delavigne 2020).

Our focus on diabetology calls for a complex methodological tool given the recent developments in the field (see section 9.2.2). Our objective is to represent the groups of speakers present in diabetology, as well as the communication situations that these speakers encounter. Indeed, as the strict dichotomy between specialists and non-specialists dissolves, in diabetology as in many specialized medical fields, this is leading to a new circulation of terms – in the sense of Humbert-Droz (2021) – between discursive communities. Consequently, terminologists need to rethink certain concepts, such as the circulation of terms between different discourse communities and the notion of expertise in light of the emergence of the patient partner, a new actor in the healthcare system[1]. To this end, we have brought together methods from strands of research in terminology and socioterminology that are concerned with these issues: textual terminology, which is based on applied research and collaboration with specialists, and socioterminology, which is based on fieldwork, oral observation and a strong sociolinguistic component (Delavigne et al. 2022).

9.2.2. *The changing medical paradigm: new grounds for terminology*

In recent years, the medical field has seen both the boundaries of expertise (Delavigne 2019) and the boundaries between specialists and laypeople blur and shift. Since the late 1950s, the gradual transformation of the doctor–patient relationship as we knew it until then has turned the caregiver–care receiver relationship on its head (Delavigne 2012; Flora 2015). There was a shift from the paternalistic Parsons model (Paganelli and Clavier 2014), in which the patient plays only a passive role and is subject to the authority of the medical profession on which they depend (Delavigne 2012; Paganelli and Clavier 2014), to the Strauss model (Paganelli and Clavier 2014), in which patients are "seen as full participants in the care process, as actors who must be informed in order to be able to actively participate in decisions that concern them" (ibid., p. 141).

1 While historically/traditionally this actor has been called "the expert patient" (Lorig et al. 1985), as this name is no longer reflective of reality, we prefer the term "patient partner" for reasons of definition and suitability to our data.

There are many reasons for the emergence of this participatory model: medical progress and improvements in living conditions and hygiene, which led to a shift from a regime of acute illnesses to one of chronic illnesses (Bureau and Hermann-Mesfen 2014), and societal transformations, such as changes in the relationship to the body and to illness, as well as the involvement of patient associations, particularly during the AIDS crisis. These changes were enforced at the institutional level thanks to legislation, such as the law of March 4, 2002 in France. Alongside legislative recognition, technological developments have contributed to the desacralization of the role of the doctor/physician and to placing the patient at the center, by making information more accessible and thereby reducing the imbalance of information between patients and medical specialists.

The patient occupies a fundamental place within this participatory model according to the logic of health democracy (Bureau and Hermann-Mesfen 2014). In a therapeutic patient education approach (World Health Organization 1998), patients are encouraged to develop skills to self-manage their illness. It is in this context that we see the emergence of the "expert patient" (Lorig et al. 1985), which the UK National Health Service defined in 1999 as "a patient who is able to make decisions in the management of their treatment, working in partnership with their doctor and other carers, and thus taking greater control over their own lives" (Flora 2010, p. 4). This redefinition of the patient's role allowed for the emergence of "lay expertise" (Akrich and Rabeharisoa 2012), which Delavigne (2019) characterizes as a "perimedical culture" – i.e. a blend of scientific, practical and personal knowledge (Delavigne et al. 2022). Communication between the communities that frequent the medical field is thus modified; it is no longer top-down from the specialist to the layperson, but takes specific forms of popularization peer-to-peer (ibid.).

These changes in the medical field have resulted in the coexistence of two forms of expertise: the scientific, biomedical expertise of the medical profession and the expertise specific to patient partners. The coexistence of these two forms of expertise creates new ways of term circulation, and the knowledge essential to patient involvement. As patients "are presumed to be involved in therapeutic choices, they must have the information necessary for this involvement, which presupposes that accurate and reliable information is made available and accessible to them. Expertise must therefore circulate, which in turn modifies language practices" (Carretier et al. 2009, p. 9).

This unprecedented context in the healthcare system questions the notion of expertise, which is undergoing profound changes as a result of the major dissemination of knowledge, particularly among people with no academic training in the subject. This is echoed by Hejoaka et al. (2019), who question the notion of experiential knowledge, which they describe as a "polysemous catch-all concept, referring to a plethora of definitions and situations experienced by patients" (ibid., p. 50), while admitting that "the boundaries between professional knowledge and patients' experiential knowledge are much more blurred" (ibid., p. 54). Given this definitional vacuum, our work seeks, at least linguistically, to identify what knowledge is circulating and how it is doing so from one discourse community to another. To this end, we have taken advantage of the links between the concepts of appropriation and circulation of notions in the lay-expert *continuum*, evoked by Hejoaka et al. (2019) to interrogate these types of expertise from a terminological point of view. We based our approach on the principle that the presence of terms characterizes the discourse of experts (Delavigne 2020), which led us to compare the linguistic practices of patient partners with those of specialists in order to assess the gap, as well as to identify their specificities.

9.2.3. *Diabetology: a suitable field for a case study*

Our choice to insert diabetology into this methodological proposal for legitimizing lay expertise is intentional. Indeed, diabetology is a pioneering field when it comes to therapeutic education: with the discovery of insulin, diabetes was one of the first conditions to evolve from an acute, deadly condition to a chronic one and thus played a key role in the paradigm shift in the healthcare system (Ménoret 2015). Because of its frequency and the changing prevalence (WHO 2020), diabetes is also a topical issue, which makes it particularly interesting.

The disciplinary framework, coupled with the unprecedented context of evolving medical systems, calls for the implementation of a specific methodology, particularly in terms of data collection, which is essential for representing the various written productions and interactions taking place in the field of diabetology.

9.3. Methodology

Our methodology is based on the hybridization of data, between written and oral interactions. By comparing specialist data with patient data, we aim to analyze the specificities, similarities and differences in terminology use by these two communities.

9.3.1. *Hybrid data*

The data for this study – currently being compiled – are of various forms: textual data, asynchronous, i.e. written texts divided into a number of sub-corpora intended to represent the different communities present in the field, and synchronous data, collected during real-life situations, in particular transcripts of real interactions between these discourse communities.

Our current corpus, from which we will draw our examples in this chapter, is composed as follows.

– Specialized sub-corpus (*spe_sc*): specialized diabetology texts. The texts included in this sub-corpus come from the *Catalogue et index des sites médicaux de langue française* (CISMeF). These texts are articles from medical journals and professional opinions, collected using keywords from the field of diabetology (such as glycemia, insulin, hypoglycemia and diabetes).

– Patient partner sub-corpus (*pp_sc*): discourses of diabetic patients involved in monitoring their disease. These texts are patient testimonials from the *Fédération française des diabétiques* (FFD) website. Other written productions (such as exchanges on forums, social media, patient productions in the context of therapeutic activities, etc.) will be incorporated in the near future, to provide a more detailed description of the patient partner.

– Sub-corpus training (informative): reference sub-corpus, used primarily to verify and compare results obtained in our two main sub-corpora. This sub-corpus is made up of final-year diploma research in therapeutic education at the University of Geneva and work by patients who have graduated in therapeutic education and are now working in training.

This corpus will be supplemented by field data; it is currently being compiled. It will be made up of transcripts of interactions from multi-actor focus groups (with patient partners, specialists, care team members, family caregivers, etc.), transcripts of semi-structured interviews, and it will be supplemented by questions to clarify certain points. Discourse analysis of exchanges, formulations and paraphrases, or the co-construction of meaning, will be scrutinized in particular during this phase of interviews and questionnaires. This plurality of data, the collection of which is inspired both by the methodologies of textual terminology and socioterminology, aims to characterize the plurality and complexity of the discourses in the field. We explored the data iteratively, in the sense that the results obtained in each group of data influenced analyses carried out on the other group. We will discuss a few examples here, based on the text corpora, as a starting point for our argument in this chapter.

9.3.2. *A contrastive analysis*

As we have said, our analyses take terms as their point of entry; they are based primarily on the principles of contrastive analysis, as conceptualized by Moirand (2007). The analyses carried out on the corpus of written productions focus on the study of semantic, lexical and formal discourse events (including frequency, distribution, contexts of occurrence, co-occurrences, semantic features, variants, etc.), some of which are exemplified below. Based on the principle that "an expert discourse, written or oral, is characterized by the presence of specific terms and phraseologies, linguistic traces of their expert knowledge" (Delavigne 2020, p. 169), we interpreted our analyses by comparing the discourse communities represented by our corpus. The objective of these contrastive analyses was to observe the modalities of appropriation of terms from the field of diabetes by patients and the semantic, syntactic and lexical consequences that result from this.

9.3.3. *A tool-based approach*

Our approach was greatly facilitated by dedicated corpus analysis tools. Since terms form the basis of our analysis, we used the term extractor TermoStat (Drouin 2003), an "automatic term extractor tool that compares specialized and non-specialized corpora in order to identify terms" (Drouin 2010). As a semi-automated system, human validation by a terminologist or specialists in the field remains indispensable (prior to this stage, the

TermoStat extraction results functioned as candidate terms). As far as the actual analysis is concerned, we mainly used concordancers, such as AntConc (Anthony 2022), and corpus managers allowing linguistic analysis, such as Sketch Engine (Kilgarriff et al. 2014) and TXM (Heiden et al. 2010).

9.4. Analysis and initial results

To illustrate our argument and to understand how a terminological approach can contribute to the characterization of expertise, we present below three analyses carried out in the corpus of written productions.

9.4.1. *Field-specific terminology in patient discourse*

Our first analysis was conducted at the lexical level. We began by drawing on the work of Delavigne (2019), who observes an abundance of medical terms in patient forums and shows that this "reservoir of data" (ibid., p. 61) enables the emergence of "perimedical cultures" (ibid.) which "[e]xpress an epistemical community that pools its knowledge, showing that it is not only on the side of the caregivers" (ibid.). The abundance of medical terms in patients' productions is thus a first step towards knowledge of a form of their expertise, insofar as the actualization of their meaning is verified in discourse. Verification and comparison of term usage in the field therefore provide possibilities for legitimizing the expertise of patient partners at the linguistic level.

A first line of thought based on terminological density can therefore be envisaged in order to question the nature and manifestations of patients' expertise. In this chapter, we will evaluate this terminological richness, based on the results of the TermoStat extraction. At this stage, our comparisons are based on the first hundred candidate terms extracted by TermoStat in each of the sub-corpora. The aim is to compare the presence of candidate terms in the two sub-corpora.

Of these 100 candidate terms, 14 are common to both corpora; of these 14, 8 are among the top 15 candidate terms extracted by TermoStat (including *insuline* (insulin), *glycémie* (glycemia), *injection* (injection)). We can therefore see that the candidate terms with the highest specificity ratio[2] are the same for both discourse communities. This leads us to conclude that the terminology most commonly used by specialists is also that most frequently used by patient partners.

This terminology, common to both sub-corpora, points to a form of patient expertise, insofar as patients use terms and concepts specific to the medical field, at least in cases where they use them in a similar way to specialists. This finding is also supported by another element of the TermoStat extraction, namely the presence of abbreviations (hypo, hyper). Dury and Picton, in an article also dealing with the medical context, postulate that using the "correct" abbreviated form for the "correct" term in a given field can be a way of showing one's membership to a professional community, as well as one's understanding of the discursive codes of that medium (Dury and Picton 2017, p. 64). In our research, the abbreviations found in *pp_sc* are also present in *spe_sc* to refer to the same term. Another interesting observation is that these abbreviations are never accompanied by their expanded form, which testifies to patients' own use of these elements and, consequently, to a mode of appropriation of these terminological elements, since it is not necessary for patients to develop or define these abbreviated forms when communicating with one another (ibid.).

9.4.2. *The absence of knowledge-rich contexts*

In our second analysis, we sought to verify the presence of information or explanations concerning the meaning of domain-specific terms in *pp_sc*. In fact, it has been shown that texts aimed at an audience with no training in the field, or at least no academic knowledge of the subject (e.g. popular texts), are distinguished by the presence of definitions and explanations for the terminology (see, for example, Hmida (2017)). Consequently, it is pertinent to question the actual presence of these explanatory elements in the discourse of expert patients, in order to see whether these patients resort to these processes of explanation or whether the terminology of the domain is familiar enough for them to use it without any explanation whatsoever.

To do this, we study the presence of knowledge-rich contexts (KRCs), a concept proposed by Meyer (2001, p. 281), which she defines as "a context

2 The specificity score is a score that helps rank candidate terms in relation to each other (Drouin 2003).

indicating at least one item of domain knowledge that could be useful for conceptual analysis. In other words, the context should indicate at least one conceptual characteristic, whether it be an attribute or a relation". KRCs can be identified in a corpus by the presence of markers that not only identify these structures, but also make explicit the relation brought about by this context (such as naming, meaning, hyperonymy, meronymy, cause/effect relationships, equivalence, etc.). For example, the sentence "*We call* insulin the hormone that allows glucose to enter the cells of the body" is a knowledge-rich context for the term insulin, with the marker "we call" providing information about the name and initial elements of definition.

So, using AntConc and Sketch Engine, we searched for possible KRCs from a pre-established list of recurrent markers in the French language, both lexico-syntactic (e.g. declensions of verbs like *appeler* (call), *nommer* (name), *dénommer* (denote), *signifier* (signify), etc., statements around i.e. searching contexts around the verb "to be" in the introduction of possible defining statements, etc.) as well as punctuation elements (such as *:* or *(...)*). In this case, the results are succinct but significant, to the extent that we note a single occurrence in the entire corpus of a marker explaining definitive information:

EXAMPLE 1.– *Et puis le temps passant, la vie a repris son cours. Je vis ce que les médecins appellent si joliment le phénomène de "lune de miel." Une belle appellation pour finalement m'expliquer que je serais plus ou moins tranquille pendant quelques années avec une glycémie plus facile à contrôler (pp_sc).*

> And then, as time went by, life resumed its course. I experienced what doctors so nicely *call* the "honeymoon" phenomenon. It is a simple way of explaining that I'll be more or less at peace for a few years with easier to manage blood sugar levels (*pp_sc*). (Our translation)

We can draw several interpretations and point to several avenues of research from these results. The first, and most obvious, is that only one marker emerged from our analysis. This shows an understanding and a form of acquisition of the terminology of doctors/physicians, since the patients sharing their experience of diabetes on the FFD website do not need to explain to their peers the terms they use or the remarks and comments they would have received from doctors/physicians.

We need to put the information contained in this segment, i.e. the description of *lune de miel* (honeymoon), into perspective, since this term is mostly used by the patients and not by specialists, according to our data (relative frequency in *spe_sc*: 0.95/million occurrences; relative frequency in *pp_sc*: 51.07/million occurrences). This observation allows us to make several hypotheses, which will be explored later, particularly in interviews.

– We can assume that this is a term specific to patient discourse, which suggests the existence of a patient-specific terminology and thus testifies to a different form of expertise.

– We can also hypothesize that the two discourses (i.e. that of the specialists and that of the patient partners) and the terms specific to them intersect and circulate between the two discourse communities, in a form of interpenetration. In fact, the higher relative frequency of *pp_sc* and the fact that the other occurrences of *lune de miel* (honeymoon) are never explicit suggest that this term is part of the patients' terminology and may be reused by healthcare professionals for the sake of clarity to facilitate the transmission of information, as the segment above suggests.

From our KRC analysis, first, we can conclude that the almost total absence of KRCs in the *pp_sc* confirms patients' mastery of the terminology. Second, these initial results suggest there is a patient terminology that circulates, probably back and forth, between different groups of speakers.

9.4.3. *The similarity of syntactic specificities*

Our last analysis aims to illustrate how a terminological approach can be used to better understand patient expertise from a linguistic perspective. It concerns the analysis of syntactic specificities. Indeed, it is widely accepted that a text is always "socially situated" (Condamines 2003, p. 32) and thereby obeys linguistic rules corresponding to the genre to which it belongs, depending on the context of production (ibid.). This is particularly true of co-occurrences and collocations, i.e. specialized lexical combinations specific to a field of specialization or with the use of a particular phraseology. It is therefore interesting to compare the use of these collocations between specialists and patient partners, in order to determine whether the latter's discourse obeys the same semantic–syntactic regularities as that of specialists in the field.

To exemplify this analysis, we have chosen the term *diabète* (diabetes) for two reasons: firstly, it is irrefutably a term of diabetology; secondly, it has a high frequency in our corpus, which makes it a significant case study. For this analysis, we focused on representative elements of phraseology, such as prepositions used with the term, verbs accompanying it and even the nouns and adjectives frequently associated with it. These elements were compared using Sketch Engine.

Figures 9.1 and 9.2 display our results in graphical form.

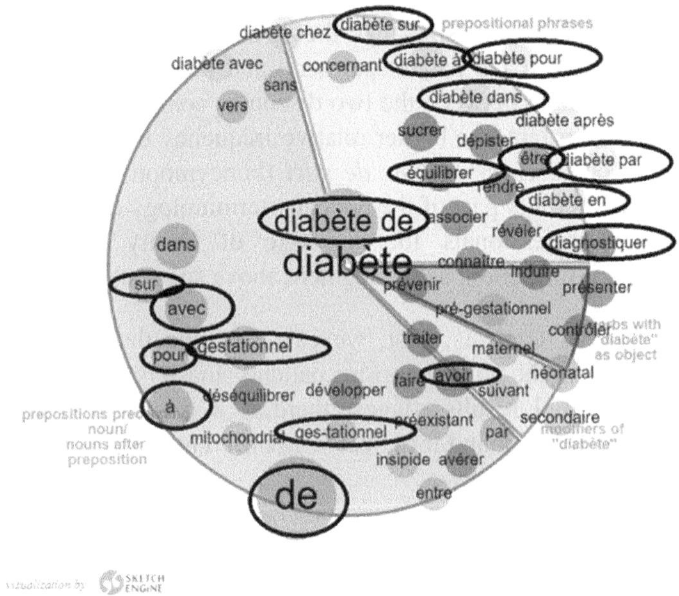

Figure 9.1. *Results from spe_sc. For a color version of this figure, see www.iste.co.uk/corroy/health.zip*

Figures 9.1 and 9.2 show that patient usage of *diabète* (diabetes) is relatively similar to specialist usage. From a purely linguistic point of view, the similarity of *diabète* (diabetes) co-occurrences tends to demonstrate that the meaning attributed to the term by both discourse communities is very similar (Heylen and Bertels 2016) and that the use made of it, in terms of phraseology, shows few differences. In both sub-corpuses, for example, we find the collocation *diabète gestationnel* (gestational diabetes). We also note that the verbs associated with diabetes by patients (e.g. *diagnostiquer* (diagnose) and *équilibrer* (balance)) echo verbs also used by specialists. The most convincing results, however, are found at the prepositional level, with similar phraseological tendencies as regards this syntactical element (e.g. *vivre avec le diabète* (living with diabetes)).

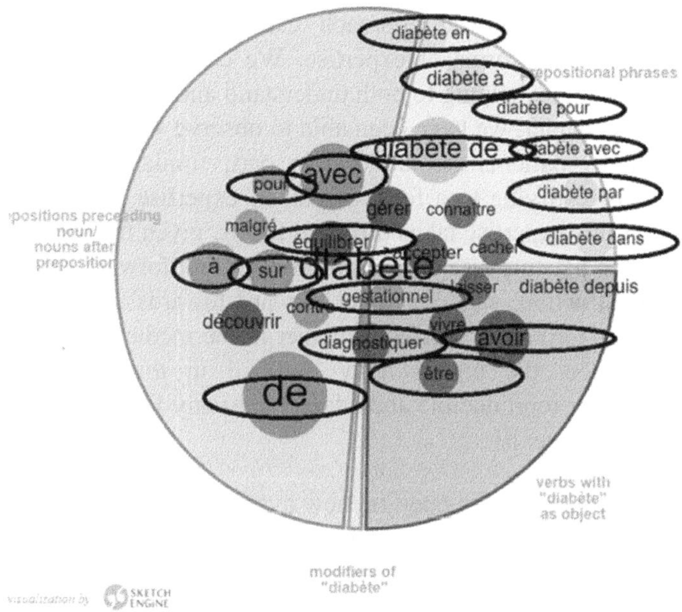

Figure 9.2. *Results from pp_sc. For a color version of this figure, see www.iste.co.uk/corroy/health.zip*

Although we are limited by the confines of this chapter, this analysis shows how linguistics can question the semantic workings of terms (here, through analysis of collocations) and grasp the similarities and specificities in terminological usage by different discourse communities. Indeed, from a linguistic point of view, the analysis of patients' syntactic tendencies regarding diabetology terms, when they correspond to specialist usage, shows a respect for their mastery of the linguistic norms of specialists. The case outlined here remains relatively simple, but now opens up the (essential) question of more or less divergent uses between specialists and patient partners: How can we measure these discrepancies and what do they reveal about patient expertise? Through our ongoing research at the University of Geneva, which extends the analyses mentioned here, we aim to uncover the mechanisms and linguistic specificities of this type of expertise.

9.5. Conclusion

By comparatively analyzing the productions and interactions at work in the discourse communities of a given field, we can understand how a terminological and linguistic approach can support reflection on uses according to different forms of expertise. We can approach lay expertise from a different angle, helping to both understand and legitimize it. From the analyses in this chapter, we have been able to observe whether the terms and concepts used by patients are, at least in part, similar to those used by specialists, thus testifying to a form of patient expertise. Our initial results also show that this expertise takes different forms, given the specificities we have observed in patients' usage. The proposal we put forward here, although still under construction, suggests ways forward towards understanding and legitimizing new forms of expertise, whether in the medical field or in other specialties. Indeed, the methodology outlined in this chapter has the advantage of being reproducible and adaptable to any field in which various forms of expertise coexist.

These preliminary results open up new avenues of research, in particular analyses during field immersion. Finally, and more generally, the descriptive approach we have presented here provides a starting point for in-depth theoretical reflection in terminology on various notions contributing to the characterization of forms of expertise. In particular, the notion of the appropriation of terms should be at the heart of these reflections, to help understand and legitimize different forms of expertise. Our proposed exploration of the subject of expertise highlights a significant issue regarding the emergence of new forms of expertise and terminology, which is ripe for further investigation.

9.6. References

Akrich, M. and Rabeharisoa, V. (2012). L'expertise profane dans les associations de patients, un outil de démocratie sanitaire. *Santé publique*, 24(1), 69–74.

Anthony, L. (2022). AntConc. Computer Software. Waseda University, Tokyo, Japan.

Bureau, E. and Hermann-Mesfen, J. (2014). Les patients contemporains face à la démocratie sanitaire. *Anthropologie & Santé. Revue internationale francophone d'anthropologie de la santé*, 8.

Carretier, J., Delavigne, V., Fervers, B. (2009). Du langage expert au langage patient : vers une prise en compte des préférences des patients dans la démarche informationnelle entre les professionnels de santé et les patients. *Sciences-Croisées*, 6.

Condamines, A. (2003). Sémantique et corpus spécialisés. Constitution de Bases de Connaissances Terminologiques. Linguistics HDR Thesis, Université Toulouse Le Mirail, Toulouse.

Delavigne, V. (2012). Peut-on traduire les mots des experts ? Un dictionnaire pour les patients atteints de cancer. In *Dictionnaires et traduction*, Heinz, M. (ed.). Frank & Timmé, Berlin.

Delavigne, V. (2019). Les mots du cancer. Le partage des termes pour l'élaboration d'une culture périmédicale. In *Comunicació, llenguatge i salut/Comunicación, lenguaje y salud. Estratègies lingüístiques per millorar la comunicació amb el pacient/Estrategias lingüísticas para mejorar la comunicación con el paciente*, Estopà, R. (ed). Pompeu Fabra University, Barcelona.

Delavigne, V. (2020). Une analyse socioterminologique de forums de patients atteints de cancer : culture périmédicale et expertise. In *Les savoirs expérientiels en santé. Fondements épistémologiques et enjeux identitaires*, Arborio, S., Hallo, A., Hejoaka, F., Simon, E. (eds). Presses universitaires de Nancy, Nancy.

Delavigne, V. and Gaudin, F. (2022). Foundational principles of socioterminology. In *Theoretical Perspectives on Terminology: Explaining Terms, Concepts and Specialized Knowledge*, Faber, P. and L'Homme, M.C. (eds). John Benjamins, Amsterdam.

Delavigne, V. and de Vecchi, D. (eds) (2021). *Termes en discours. Entreprises et organisations*. Presses de la Sorbonne Nouvelle, Paris.

Delavigne, V., Picton, A., Thibert, E. (2022). Socioterminologie et terminologie textuelle : l'expertise en questions. *SHS Web of Conferences*, 138(04012), 1–15 [Online]. Available at: https://hal.science/hal-03717050/document.

Drouin, P. (2003). Term extraction using non-technical corpora as a point of leverage. *Terminology*, 9(1), 99–117.

Drouin, P. (2010). Guide de l'utilisateur. TermoStat 3.0 [Online]. Available at: http://termostat.ling.umontreal.ca/doc_termostat/doc_termostat_en.html.

Dury, P. and Picton, A. (2017). Diastratic variation in language for specific purposes. Observations from the analysis of two corpora. In *Multiple Perspectives in Terminological Variation. Terminology and Lexicography Research and Practice*, Drouin, P., Francœur, A., Humbley, J., Picton, A. (eds). John Benjamins Publishing Company, Amsterdam, 57–79.

Flora, L. (2010). De la métamorphose des approches de la santé, à l'émergence de l'usager expert, au patient formateur. *Actes du congrès de l'Actualité de la recherche en éducation et en formation (AREF)*. Université de Genève, September [Online]. Available at: https://plone.unige.ch/aref2010/communications-orales/premiers-auteurs-en-g/De%20la%20metamorphose.pdf/view.

Flora, L. (2015). Du patient "passif" au patient expert. In *Regards croisés sur l'idée de guérison et de rétablissement en santé mentale*, Déchamp-Le Roux, C. and Rafael, F. (eds). John Libbey Eurotext Limited, Toulouse.

Heiden, S., Magué, J.P., Pincemin, B. (2010). TXM : une plateforme logicielle open-source pour la textométrie – conception et développement. In *10th International Conference on the Statistical Analysis of Textual Data - JADT 2010*, June, Rome, 1021–1032 [Online]. Available at: https://shs.hal.science/halshs-00549779.

Hejoaka, F., Simon, E. Halloy, A., Arborio, S. (eds) (2019). Définir les savoirs expérentiels en santé : une revue de la littérature en sciences humaines et sociales. In *Les savoirs expérientiels en santé : fondements épistémologiques et enjeux identitaires*. Presses universitaires de Nancy, Nancy.

Heylen, K. and Bertels, A. (2016). Sémantique distributionnelle en linguistique de corpus. *Langages*, 201(1), 51–64.

Hmida, F. (2017). Identification et exploitation de contextes riches en connaissances pour l'aide à la traduction terminologique. PhD Thesis, Université de Nantes, Nantes.

Humbert-Droz, J. (2021). Définir la déterminologisation : approche outillée en corpus comparable dans le domaine de la physique des particules. PhD Thesis, Université de Genève, Geneva.

Kilgarriff, A., Baisa, V., Bušta, J., Jakubíček, M., Kovář, V., Michelfeit, J., Rychlý, P., Suchomel, V. (2014). The sketch engine: Ten years. *Lexicography*, 1, 7–36.

Lorig, K., Lubeck, D., Kraines, R.G., Seleznick, M., Holman, H.R. (1985). Outcomes of self-help education for patients with arthritis. *Arthritis and Rheumatism*, 28(6), 680–685.

Ménoret, M. (2015). La prescription d'autonomie en médecine. *Anthropologie & Santé. Revue internationale francophone d'anthropologie de la santé*, 10.

Meyer, I. (ed.) (2001). Extracting knowledge-rich contexts for terminography: A conceptual and methodological framework. In *Recent Advances in Computational Terminology*. John Benjamins Publishing Company, Amsterdam.

Moirand, S. and Tréguer-Felten, G. (2007). Des mots de la langue aux discours spécialisés, des acteurs sociaux à la part culturelle du langage : raisons et conséquences de ces déplacements. *ASp. la revue du GERAS*, 51–52, 7–33.

Paganelli, C. and Clavier, V. (2014). S'informer via des médias sociaux de santé. Quelle place pour les experts ? *Le Temps des médias*, 23.

Picton, A. and Condamines, A. (2022). Textual terminology. Origins, principles and new challenges. In *Theoretical Perspectives on Terminology: Explaining Terms, Concepts and Specialized Knowledge*, Faber, P. and L'Homme, M.C. (eds). John Benjamins Publishing Company, Amsterdam.

WHO (1998). Therapeutic patient education: Continuing education programmes for healthcare providers in the field of prevention of chronic diseases. Report, WHO Working Group, Geneva.

WHO (2020). Diabetes. Report, WHO, Geneva.

List of Authors

Christelle CHAUZAL-LARGUIER
Communication et Sociétés
Université Clermont Auvergne
Clermont-Ferrand
France

Laurence CORROY
CREM
Université de Lorraine
Nancy
France

Stéphanie DEBRAY
AHP-PReST
Université de Lorraine
Nancy
France

Valérie DELAVIGNE
CLESTHIA
Université Sorbonne Nouvelle
Paris
France

Lucile DESMOULINS
DICEN-Idf
Université Gustave Eiffel
Paris-Nanterre
France

Oihana HUSSON
CIMEOS
Université de Bourgogne
Dijon
France

Alexis MEYER
Communication et Sociétés
Université Clermont Auvergne
Clermont-Ferrand
France

Alexandra MICCICHE
Centre de recherches Mondes modernes et contemporains
Université libre de Bruxelles
and
HiSI
Université de Namur
Belgium

Aurélie PICTON
TIM
Université de Toulouse
Jean-Jaurès
France
and
OLST
Université de Montréal
Canada

Sylvie PIERRE
CREM
Université de Lorraine
Nancy
France

Aurélie POURREZ
CREM
Université de Lorraine
Nancy
France

Émilie ROCHE
CERLIS
Université Sorbonne Nouvelle
Paris
France

Corinne ROCHETTE
CleRMa
Université Clermont Auvergne
Clermont-Ferrand
France

Baptiste SCHUMMER
CERAPS
Université de Lille
France

Emma THIBERT
TIM
Université de Toulouse
Jean-Jaurès
France

Index

E, F

G, H

I, J

K, L

M, O

P, R

S, T, W, X

Other titles from

iSTE

in

Health Engineering and Society

2024

SARAZIN Marianne
Artificial Intelligence in Health
(Technological Prospects and Social Applications Set – Volume 7)

2023

BEYALA Laure
Digital Therapy: The New Age of Healthcare
(Technological Prospects and Social Applications Set – Volume 6)

CORROY Laurence, CHAUZAL-LARGUIER Christelle
Patients, Caregivers and Doctors: Devices, Issues and Representations
(Communication and Health Set – Volume 1)

SOMMER Pascal, DEBRET Romain
The Elasticity of Life: From Tissues to Humans

2022

ASSAILLY Jean-Pascal
Child Psychology: Developments in Knowledge and Theoretical Models
(Health and Patients Set – Volume 3)

CHAABANE Sondès, COUSEIN Etienne, WIESER Philippe
Healthcare Systems: Challenges and Opportunities

PAGANELLI Céline, CLAVIER Viviane
Information Practices and Knowledge in Health
(Health and Patients Set – Volume 5)

SALGUES Bruno, BARNOUIN Jacques
The Covid-19 Crisis: From a Question of an Epidemic to a Societal Questioning
(Health and Patients Set – Volume 4)

2021

BÉRANGER Jérôme
Societal Responsibility of Artificial Intelligence: Towards an Ethical and Eco-responsible AI
(Technological Prospects and Social Applications Set – Volume 4)

CORDELIER Benoit, GALIBERT Olivier
Digital Health Communications
(Technological Prospects and Social Applications Set – Volume 5)

NADOT Michel
Discipline of Nursing: Three-time Knowledge

2020

BARBET Jacques, FOUCQUIER Adrien, THOMAS Yves
Therapeutic Progress in Oncology: Towards a Revolution in Cancer Therapy?
(Health and Patients Set – Volume 2)

MORILLON Laurent, CLAVIER Viviane
Health Research Practices in a Digital Context
(Health Information Set – Volume 4)

PAILLIART Isabelle
New Territories in Health
(Health Information Set – Volume 3)

2019

CLAVIER Viviane, DE OLIVEIRA Jean-Philippe
Food and Health: Actor Strategies in Information and Communication
(Health Information Set – Volume 2)

PIZON Frank
Health Education and Prevention
(Health and Patients Set – Volume 1)

2018

HUARD Pierre
The Management of Chronic Diseases: Organizational Innovation and Efficiency

PAGANELLI Céline
Confidence and Legitimacy in Health Information and Communication
(Health Information Set – Volume 1)

2017

PICARD Robert
Co-design in Living Labs for Healthcare and Independent Living: Concepts, Methods and Tools

2015

BÉRANGER Jérôme
Medical Information Systems Ethics

Printed and bound by CPI Group (UK) Ltd, Croydon, CR0 4YY

28/07/2026

14931341-0002